U0530030

新丝路"中文+职业技能"系列教材编写委员会
（电子商务）

总策划：马箭飞　谢永华

策　划：宋永波　孙雁飞

顾　问：朱志平（北京师范大学）

　　　　林秀琴（首都师范大学）

　　　　宋继华（北京师范大学）

总主编：谢永华　杜曾慧

语言类主编：杨立力

专业类主编：沈新淇

语言类副主编：杜　娟　李　晖

专业类副主编：杨　俊　谈　璐　谢吉刚

项目组长：郭凤岚

项目副组长：付彦白

项目成员：郭　冰　武传霞　齐　琰　赫　栗　李金梅

新丝路"中文+职业技能"系列教材
New Silk Road "Chinese + Vocational Skills" Series

中文+电子商务
Chinese + E-commerce

中级 Intermediate

新丝路"中文+职业技能"系列教材编写委员会 编

北京语言大学出版社
BEIJING LANGUAGE AND CULTURE UNIVERSITY PRESS

© 2023 北京语言大学出版社，社图号 23245

图书在版编目（CIP）数据

中文 + 电子商务 . 中级 ／ 新丝路"中文 + 职业技能"系列教材编写委员会编 . -- 北京：北京语言大学出版社，2023.12

新丝路"中文 + 职业技能"系列教材

ISBN 978-7-5619-6460-6

Ⅰ.①中… Ⅱ.①新… Ⅲ.①汉语－对外汉语教学－教材②电子商务－教材 Ⅳ.① H195.4 ② F713.36

中国国家版本馆 CIP 数据核字（2023）第 229118 号

中文 + 电子商务（中级）
ZHONGWEN + DIANZI SHANGWU (ZHONGJI)

排版制作：	北京创艺涵文化发展有限公司
责任印制：	周 燚

出版发行：	北京语言大学出版社
社　　址：	北京市海淀区学院路 15 号，100083
网　　址：	www.blcup.com
电子信箱：	service@blcup.com
电　　话：	编 辑 部　8610-82303647/3592/3395
	国内发行　8610-82303650/3591/3648
	海外发行　8610-82303365/3080/3668
	北语书店　8610-82303653
	网购咨询　8610-82303908
印　　刷：	北京富资园科技发展有限公司

版　　次：	2023 年 12 月第 1 版	**印　　次：**	2023 年 12 月第 1 次印刷
开　　本：	889 毫米 × 1194 毫米　1/16	**印　　张：**	10
字　　数：	181 千字		
定　　价：	98.00 元		

PRINTED IN CHINA

凡有印装质量问题，本社负责调换。售后 QQ 号 1367565611，电话 010-82303590

编写说明

新丝路"中文+职业技能"系列教材是把中文作为第二语言，结合专业和职业的专门用途、职业用途的中文教材，不是专业理论教材，不是一般意义的通用综合中文教材。本系列教材定位为职场生存中文教材、立体式技能型语言教材。教材研发的目标是既要满足学习者一般中文环境下的基本交际需求，又要满足学习者职业学习需求和职场工作需求。它和普通的国际中文教材的区别不在语法，而在词汇的专门化程度，在中文的用途、使用场合、应用范围。目前，专门用途、职业用途的中文教材在语言分类和研究成果上几近空白，本系列教材的成功研发开创了中文学习的新视野、新领域、新方向，将"中文+职业技能+X等级证书"真正融合，使学习者在学习中文的同时，也可通过实践掌握职业技能，从而获得X等级证书。

适用对象

本系列教材将适用对象定位为双零基础（零语言基础、零技能基础）的来华学习中文和先进技能的长期或者短期进修生，可满足初、中、高各层次专业课程的教学需要。教材亦可供海内外相关的培训课程及"走出去"的中资企业培训本土化员工使用。

结构规模

本系列教材采取专项语言技能与职业技能训练相结合的中文教学及教材编写模式。教材选择当前热门的物流管理、汽车服务工程技术、电子商务、机电一体化、计算机网络技术、酒店管理等六个专业，培养各专业急需急用的技术岗位人才。每个专业教材均包括初、中、高级三册。每一册都配有专业视频教学资源，还附有"视频脚本""参考答案"等配套资源。

编写理念

本系列教材将词语进行分类，区分普通词语和专业词语，以通用语料为基础，以概念性、行为性词语为主，不脱离职场情境讨论分级，做到控制词汇量，控制工作场景，控制交流内容与方式，构建语义框架。将语言的分级和专业的分级科学地融合，是实现本系列教材成功编写的关键。

教材目标

语言技能目标：

初级阶段，能熟练掌握基础通用词语和职场的常用专业词语，能使用简短句子进行简单的生活及工作交流。中级阶段，能听懂工作场合简单的交谈与发言，明白大意，把握基本情况，能就工作中重要的话题用简单的话与人沟通。高级阶段，能听懂工作场合一般的交谈与发言，抓住主要内容和关键信息，使用基本交际策略与人交流、开展工作，能初步了解与交际活动相关的文化因素，掌握与交际有关的一般文化背景知识，能排除交际时遇到的文化障碍。交际能力层次的递进实现从初级的常规礼节、基本生活及工作的交流能力，到中级的简单的服务流程信息交流能力，最后达到高级的复杂信息的交流和特情处理的能力。

职业技能目标：

以满足岗位需求为目标，将遴选出的当前热门的专业工作岗位分为初、中、高三级。物流管理专业初、中、高级对应的岗位分别是物流员、物流经理、物流总监；汽车服务工程技术专业初、中、高级对应的岗位分别是汽车机电维修工、汽车服务顾问、技术总监；电子商务专业初、中、高级对应的岗位分别是电子商务运营助理、电子商务运营员、电子商务客服；机电一体化专业初、中、高级对应的岗位分别是机电操作工、机电调整工、机电维修工；计算机网络技术专业初、中、高级对应的岗位分别是宽带运维工程师、网络运维专员、网络管理员；酒店管理专业初、中、高级对应的岗位分别是前厅基层接待员、前厅主管、前厅经理。每个专业分解出三十个工作场景/任务，学习者在学习后能够全面掌握此岗位的概况及基本程序，实现语言学习和专业操作的双重目标。

编写原则

1. 语言知识技能与专业知识技能并进，满足当前热门的、急需急用的岗位需求。
2. 渐进分化，综合贯通，拆解难点，分而治之。
3. 语言知识与专业知识科学、高效复现，语言技能与专业技能螺旋式上升，职场情境、语义框架、本体输入方式相互配合。
4. 使用大量的图片和视频，实现专业知识和技能呈现形式可视化。
5. 强化专业岗位实操性技能。本系列教材配有专业技术教学的视频，突出展示专业岗位的实操性技能，语言学习难度与技能掌握难度的不匹配可通过实操性强的视频和实训环节来补充。

特色追求

本系列教材从初级最基础的语音知识学习和岗位认知开始，将"中文＋职业技能"融入在工作场景对话中，把工作分解成一个个任务，用图片认知的方式解决专业词语的认知问题，用视频展示的方法解决学习者掌握中文词语与专业技能的不匹配问题，注重技能的实操性，注重"在做中学"。每一单元都设置了"学以致用"板块，目的不仅仅是解决本单元任务的词语认知问题，更是将学习的目标放在"能听""能用""能模仿说出"上。我们力争通过大量图片的使用和配套视频的展示，将教材打造成立体式、技能型语言教材，方便学习者能够更好地自主学习。

使用建议

1. 本系列教材每个专业分为初、中、高级三册，每册10单元，初级每单元建议8～10课时完成，中级10～12课时完成，高级12～14课时完成。

2. 教材注释和说明着力于简明扼要，注重实操性，注重听说技能培养，对于教材涉及的语法知识，教师可视情况予以细化和补充。

3. "单元实训"板块可以在课文和语言点学完之后作为课堂练习使用，建议2课时完成。教师要带着学习者按照实训步骤一步步完成，实训步骤不要求学习者能够看懂、读懂，重要的是教师要引领操作，实现学习者掌握专业技能的目标。

4. "单元小结"板块是对整个单元关键词语和核心内容的总结，对于这部分内容，教师要进行听说练习，以便更好地帮助学习者了解本单元的核心工作任务。

5. 教师上课时要充分利用教材设计的练习，引导学习者多听多练，听说结合，学做合一。

6. 教师要带着学习者熟练诵读课文，要求学习者把每课的关键词语和句子、课堂用语背诵下来。

特别感谢

感谢教育部中外语言交流合作中心将新丝路"中文＋职业技能"系列教材列为重点研发项目，为我们教材编写增添了动力和责任感。教材编写委员会负责整套教材的规划、设计与编写协调，并先后召开上百次讨论会，对每册教材的课文编写、体例安排、注释说明、练习设计、图片选择、视频制作等进行全方位的评估、讨论和审定。感谢编写委员会成员和所有编者高度的敬业精神、精益求精的编写态度，以及所投入的热情和精力、付出的心血与智慧。感谢关注本系列教材并贡献宝贵意见的国际中文教育教学界专家和全国各地的同人。

新丝路"中文＋职业技能"系列教材编写委员会

2023年4月

Compilation Instructions

The New Silk Road "Chinese + Vocational Skills" is a series of Chinese textbooks for specialized and vocational purposes that combine professional and vocational technologies with Chinese as a second language. Instead of being specialized theoretical textbooks, or comprehensive or universal Chinese textbooks in a general sense, this series is intended to be Chinese textbooks for career survival, and three-dimensional skills-based language textbooks. The textbooks are developed with a view to meeting students' basic communication needs in general Chinese environment, and their professional learning needs and workplace demands as well. They are different from ordinary Chinese textbooks for foreigners in the degree of specialization of vocabulary, in the purpose, usage occasion, and application scope of Chinese (not in grammar). At present, Chinese textbooks for specialized and vocational purposes are virtually non-existent in terms of language classification and research results, so the successful development of this series has opened up new horizons, new fields and new directions for Chinese learning, and virtually integrated "Chinese + Vocational Skills + X-Level Certificates", which enables students to practically master vocational skills and obtain X-level certificates while learning Chinese.

Applicable Targets

This series is targeted at long-term or short-term students who come to China to learn Chinese and advanced skills with zero language basis and zero skill basis, which can meet the teaching needs of the elementary, intermediate and advanced specialized courses. This series can also be used for relevant training courses at home and abroad and for Chinese-funded enterprises that "go global" to train local employees.

Structure and Scale

This series adopts a Chinese teaching and textbook compilation model combining special language skills and vocational skills training. The series includes the textbooks for six popular majors such as logistics management, automotive service engineering technology, e-commerce, mechatronics, computer networking technology, and hotel management to cultivate technical talents in urgent need. The textbooks for each major consist of the textbooks at the elementary, intermediate and advanced levels. Each textbook is equipped with professional video teaching resources, and "video scripts", "reference answers" and other supporting resources as well.

Compilation Concept

This series classifies the vocabulary into general vocabulary and specialized vocabulary. Based on the general vocabulary, it focuses on conceptual and behavioral words, not deviating from workplace situations, so as to control the vocabulary, work scenarios and content and means of communication, and build the semantic framework. The scientific integration of language classification and specialty classification is the key to the successful compilation of textbooks.

Textbook Objectives

Language Skill Objectives

For students at the elementary level, they are trained to be familiar with basic general vocabulary and common specialized vocabulary in the workplace, and be able to use short sentences for simple communication in life and at work. For those at the intermediate level, they are trained to understand simple conversations and speeches in the workplace, comprehend the main ideas, grasp the basic situations, and communicate with others in simple words on important topics at work. For those at the advanced level, they are trained to be able to understand general conversations and speeches in the workplace, grasp the main content and key information, use basic communication strategies to communicate with others and carry out the work, have a preliminary understanding of cultural factors related to communication activities, master the general communication-related cultural background knowledge, and overcome cultural barriers encountered during communication. The progression in level of communicative competence helps them to leap forward from routine etiquette, basic communication in life and at work at the elementary level, to simple information exchange of service processes at the intermediate level, and finally to complex information exchange and handling of special circumstances at the advanced level.

Vocational Skill Objectives

To meet job requirements at the elementary, intermediate and advanced levels, the professional positions that are most urgently needed overseas are selected. The positions corresponding to logistics management at the elementary, intermediate and advanced levels are logistics staff, logistics managers and logistics directors; the positions corresponding to automotive service engineering technology at the elementary, intermediate and advanced levels are automotive electromechanical maintenance staff, automotive service consultants and technical directors; the positions corresponding to e-commerce at the elementary, intermediate and advanced levels are electronic operation assistants, e-commerce operators and e-commerce customer service staff; the positions corresponding to mechatronics at the elementary, intermediate and advanced levels are mechanical and electrical operators, mechanical and electrical adjusters, and mechanical and electrical maintenance staff; the positions corresponding to computer networking techology at the elementary, intermediate and advanced levels are broadband operation and maintenance engineers, network operation and maintenance specialists, and network administrators; the positions corresponding to hotel management at the elementary, intermediate and advanced levels are lobby receptionists, lobby supervisors and lobby managers. Through 30 work scenarios/tasks set for each major, learners can fully grasp the general situations and basic procedures of the position after learning, and achieve the dual goals of language learning and professional operation.

Principles of Compilation

1. Language knowledge skills and professional knowledge skills go hand in hand to meet the demands of current popular and urgently needed job positions;

2. It makes progressive differentiation and comprehensive integration, breaking down, dividing and conquering difficult points;

3. Language knowledge and professional knowledge recur scientifically and efficiently, language skills and professional skills spiral upward, and the situational stage, semantic framework, and ontology input methods cooperate with each other;

4. Professional knowledge and skills are visualized, using a lot of pictures and videos;

5. It strengthens the practical skills in professional positions. This series of textbooks is equipped with videos of professional technical training, highlighting the practical skills for professional positions. It addresses the mismatch between the difficulty of language learning and that of mastering skills by supplementing with practical videos and practical training.

Characteristic Pursuit

Starting from the basic phonetic knowledge learning and job cognition at the elementary level, this series integrates "Chinese + Vocational Skills" into the working scene dialogues, breaking down the job into various tasks, solving lexical students' problems by means of picture cognition, solving the problem of the mismatch between students' mastery of Chinese vocabulary and professional skills by means of displaying videos, stressing the practicality of skills, and focusing on "learning by doing". Each unit has a "Practicing What You Have Learnt" module, which not only solves the problem of lexical cognition of this unit, but also takes "being able to comprehend", "being able to use" and "being able to imitate" as the learning objectives. We strive to use a large number of pictures and display supporting videos to build the textbooks into three-dimensional skills-based language teaching materials, so that learners can learn more independently.

Recommendations for Use

1. Each major of this series consists of three volumes at the elementary, intermediate, and advanced levels, with 10 units in each volume. For each unit, it is recommended to be completed in 8-10 class hours at the elementary level, 10-12 class hours at the intermediate level, and 12-14 class hours at the advanced level.

2. The notes and explanations in the textbooks focus on conciseness, practicality, and the training of listening and speaking skills. The grammar knowledge in the textbooks can be detailed and supplemented by teachers as the case may be.

3. "Unit Practical Training" module can be used as a classroom exercise after the texts and language points, preferably to be completed in two class hours. Teachers should guide students to complete the training tasks step by step. Students are not required to read and understand the training steps. It is important that teachers guide students to achieve the goal of mastering professional skills.

4. "Unit Summary" module summarizes the keywords and core content of the entire unit. Through listening and speaking exercises, this part can better help learners understand the core tasks of this unit.

5. Teachers should make full use of the exercises designed in the textbooks during class, and guide students to listen more and practice more, combine listening and speaking, and integrate learning with practice.

6. Teachers should guide students to proficiently read the texts aloud, asking them to recite the keywords, sentences and classroom expressions in each unit.

Acknowledgements

We are grateful to the Center for Language Education and Cooperation of the Ministry of Education for listing the New Silk Road "Chinese + Vocational Skills" series as a key research and development project, which adds motivation and a sense of responsibility to our textbook compilation. The Textbook Compilation Committee is responsible for the planning, design, compilation and coordination of the entire set of textbooks, and has held hundreds of seminars to conduct a comprehensive evaluation, discussion, examination and approval of text compilation, style arrangement, notes and explanations, exercise design, picture selection, and video production of each textbook. We are indebted to the members of the Compilation Committee and all compilers for their professional dedication, unwavering pursuit of perfection in the compilation, as well as their enthusiasm, hard work and wisdom. We are thankful to the experts in international Chinese language education and colleagues from all over the country who have kept a close eye on this series and contributed their valuable opinions.

Compilation Committee of New Silk Road "Chinese + Vocational Skills" Series

April 2023

rénwù jièshào
人物介绍
Introduction to Characters

zǒngjīnglǐ
总经理
General Manager

yùnyíng zǒngjiān
运营总监
Operations Director

yùnyíng zhùlǐ
运营助理
Operations Assistant

měigōng
美工
Art Designer

kèfú
客服
Customer Service

cāngguǎn
仓管
Warehouse Keeper

9

语法术语及缩略形式参照表
Abbreviations of Grammar Terms

Grammar Terms in Chinese	Grammar Terms in Pinyin	Grammar Terms in English	Abbreviations
名词	míngcí	noun	n.
专有名词	zhuānyǒu míngcí	proper noun	pn.
代词	dàicí	pronoun	pron.
数词	shùcí	numeral	num.
量词	liàngcí	measure word	m.
数量词	shùliàngcí	quantifier	q.
动词	dòngcí	verb	v.
助动词	zhùdòngcí	auxiliary	aux.
形容词	xíngróngcí	adjective	adj.
副词	fùcí	adverb	adv.
介词	jiècí	preposition	prep.
连词	liáncí	conjunction	conj.
助词	zhùcí	particle	part.
拟声词	nǐshēngcí	onomatopoeia	onom.
叹词	tàncí	interjection	int.
前缀	qiánzhuì	prefix	pref.
后缀	hòuzhuì	suffix	suf.
成语	chéngyǔ	idiom	idm.
短语	duǎnyǔ	phrase	phr.
主语	zhǔyǔ	subject	S
谓语	wèiyǔ	predicate	P
宾语	bīnyǔ	object	O
定语	dìngyǔ	attributive	Attrib
状语	zhuàngyǔ	adverbial	Adverb
补语	bǔyǔ	complement	C

CONTENTS 目录

第一单元　虾皮处罚规则　Unit 1　Punishment Rules of Shopee　1

第一部分　课文　Texts　2
　一、热身 Warm-up　2
　二、课文 Texts　4
　三、视听说 Viewing, Listening and Speaking　6
　四、学以致用 Practicing What You Have Learnt　7
　五、小知识 Tips　8

第二部分　汉字　Chinese Characters　9
　一、汉字知识 Knowledge about Chinese Characters　9
　　1. 汉字的笔画（1） Strokes of Chinese characters (1)
　　　一 丨 丿 ㇏
　　2. 汉字的笔顺（1） Stroke orders of Chinese characters (1)
　　　先横后竖 Horizontal strokes before vertical strokes
　　　先撇后捺 Left-falling strokes before right-falling strokes
　二、汉字认读与书写 The Recognition and Writing of Chinese Characters　10

第三部分　日常用语　Daily Expressions　10

第四部分　单元实训　Unit Practical Training　10
　电商平台处罚规则案例分析 Case Analysis of Punishment Rules of E-commerce Platforms　10

第五部分　单元小结　Unit Summary　11

第二单元　激励政策　Unit 2　Incentive Policies　15

第一部分　课文　Texts　16
　一、热身 Warm-up　16
　二、课文 Texts　17
　三、视听说 Viewing, Listening and Speaking　20
　四、学以致用 Practicing What You Have Learnt　21
　五、小知识 Tips　22

第二部分　汉字　Chinese Characters　23
　一、汉字知识 Knowledge about Chinese Characters　23

I

        1. 汉字的笔画（2） Strokes of Chinese characters (2)
          丶 フ ㄴ ノ
        2. 汉字的笔顺（2） Stroke orders of Chinese characters (2)
          先上后下 Upper strokes before lower strokes
          先左后右 Left-side strokes before right-side strokes
    二、汉字认读与书写 The Recognition and Writing of Chinese Characters   23
第三部分 日常用语 **Daily Expressions**   23
第四部分 单元实训 **Unit Practical Training**   24
    电商平台激励政策案例分析 Case Analysis of Incentive Policies of E-commerce Platforms 24
第五部分 单元小结 **Unit Summary**   25

第三单元　爆款打造　Unit 3　The Shaping of Hot-Selling Products　27

第一部分 课文 **Texts**   28
    一、热身 Warm-up   28
    二、课文 Texts   30
    三、视听说 Viewing, Listening and Speaking   32
    四、学以致用 Practicing What You Have Learnt   33
    五、小知识 Tips   34
第二部分 汉字 **Chinese Characters**   35
    一、汉字知识 Knowledge about Chinese Characters   35
        1. 汉字的笔画（3） Strokes of Chinese characters (3)
          ⺄ 丿 ㇏ ㄴ
        2. 汉字的笔顺（3） Stroke orders of Chinese characters (3)
          先中间后两边 Strokes in the middle before those on both sides
          先外边后里边 Outside strokes before inside strokes
    二、汉字认读与书写 The Recognition and Writing of Chinese Characters   35
第三部分 日常用语 **Daily Expressions**   36
第四部分 单元实训 **Unit Practical Training**   36
    店铺爆款打造策划 Stores' Planning of Shaping Hot-Selling Products   36
第五部分 单元小结 **Unit Summary**   37

第四单元　标题优化　Unit 4　Title Optimization　39

第一部分 课文 **Texts**   40
    一、热身 Warm-up   40
    二、课文 Texts   42

三、视听说 Viewing, Listening and Speaking		44
四、学以致用 Practicing What You Have Learnt		45
五、小知识 Tips		45

第二部分 汉字　Chinese Characters　46

　　一、汉字知识 Knowledge about Chinese Characters　46

　　　　1. 汉字的笔画（4） Strokes of Chinese characters (4)
　　　　　丶丨㇆㇇

　　　　2. 汉字的笔顺（4） Stroke orders of Chinese characters (4)
　　　　　先外后里再封口 Outside strokes before inside strokes, and then sealing strokes

　　二、汉字认读与书写 The Recognition and Writing of Chinese Characters　47

第三部分 日常用语　Daily Expressions　47

第四部分 单元实训　Unit Practical Training　47

　　产品标题优化 Product Title Optimization　47

第五部分 单元小结　Unit Summary　48

第五单元　主图优化　Unit 5　Main Image Optimization　51

第一部分 课文　Texts　52

　　一、热身 Warm-up　52
　　二、课文 Texts　54
　　三、视听说 Viewing, Listening and Speaking　56
　　四、学以致用 Practicing What You Have Learnt　57
　　五、小知识 Tips　57

第二部分 汉字　Chinese Characters　58

　　一、汉字知识 Knowledge about Chinese Characters　58

　　　　1. 汉字的笔画（5） Strokes of Chinese characters (5)
　　　　　㇏㇀㇚乙

　　　　2. 汉字的结构（1） Structures of Chinese characters (1)
　　　　　独体结构 Independent structure

　　二、汉字认读与书写 The Recognition and Writing of Chinese Characters　59

第三部分 日常用语　Daily Expressions　59

第四部分 单元实训　Unit Practical Training　59

　　产品主图优化与点击率调研 Research on Main Image Optimization and Click-through Rate　59

第五部分 单元小结　Unit Summary　60

III

第六单元　站内引流　Unit 6　On-site Traffic Driving　63

第一部分　课文　Texts　64
- 一、热身 Warm-up　64
- 二、课文 Texts　66
- 三、视听说 Viewing, Listening and Speaking　68
- 四、学以致用 Practicing What You Have Learnt　69
- 五、小知识 Tips　70

第二部分　汉字　Chinese Characters　71
- 一、汉字知识　Knowledge about Chinese Characters　71
  1. 汉字的笔画（6） Strokes of Chinese characters (6)
     乛 ㄋ
  2. 汉字的结构（2） Structures of Chinese characters (2)
     品字形结构　品-shaped structure
- 二、汉字认读与书写 The Recognition and Writing of Chinese Characters　71

第三部分　日常用语　Daily Expressions　71

第四部分　单元实训　Unit Practical Training　72
电商平台站内引流广告的使用
Use of On-site Traffic Driving Advertisements on E-commerce Platforms　72

第五部分　单元小结　Unit Summary　73

第七单元　店铺促销　Unit 7　Sales Promotion of Stores　75

第一部分　课文　Texts　76
- 一、热身 Warm-up　76
- 二、课文 Texts　77
- 三、视听说 Viewing, Listening and Speaking　79
- 四、学以致用 Practicing What You Have Learnt　80
- 五、小知识 Tips　80

第二部分　汉字　Chinese Characters　81
- 一、汉字知识 Knowledge about Chinese Characters　81
  1. 汉字的笔画（7） Strokes of Chinese characters (7)
     ㄅ 乁
  2. 汉字的结构（3） Structures of Chinese characters (3)
     上下结构 Top-bottom structure
     上中下结构 Top-middle-bottom structure
- 二、汉字认读与书写 The Recognition and Writing of Chinese Characters　82

第三部分　日常用语　Daily Expressions　82

第四部分 单元实训	**Unit Practical Training**	82
店铺促销 Sales Promotion of Stores		82
第五部分 单元小结	**Unit Summary**	83

第八单元　活动策划　Unit 8　Activity Planning　85

第一部分 课文	**Texts**	86
一、热身 Warm-up		86
二、课文 Texts		87
三、视听说 Viewing, Listening and Speaking		90
四、学以致用 Practicing What You Have Learnt		91
五、小知识 Tips		92
第二部分 汉字	**Chinese Characters**	93
一、汉字知识 Knowledge about Chinese Characters		93

1. 汉字的笔画（8）　Strokes of Chinese characters (8)
   乚 乙

2. 汉字的结构（4）　Structures of Chinese characters (4)
   左右结构 Left-right structure
   左中右结构 Left-middle-right structure

二、汉字认读与书写 The Recognition and Writing of Chinese Characters		93
第三部分 日常用语	**Daily Expressions**	93
第四部分 单元实训	**Unit Practical Training**	94
电商平台活动策划 Activity Planning of E-commerce Platforms		94
第五部分 单元小结	**Unit Summary**	95

第九单元　优质客服　Unit 9　High Quality Customer Service　98

第一部分 课文	**Texts**	98
一、热身 Warm-up		100
二、课文 Texts		102
三、视听说 Viewing, Listening and Speaking		103
四、学以致用 Practicing What You Have Learnt		103
五、小知识 Tips		104
第二部分 汉字	**Chinese Characters**	104
一、汉字知识 Knowledge about Chinese Characters		104

1. 汉字的笔画（9）　Strokes of Chinese characters (9)

2. 汉字的结构（5） Structures of Chinese characters (5)
  全包围结构 Fully-enclosed structure
  半包围结构 Semi-enclosed structure

  二、汉字认读与书写 The Recognition and Writing of Chinese Characters   105

第三部分 日常用语 **Daily Expressions**   105

第四部分 单元实训 **Unit Practical Training**   106

  电商优质客服 High Quality Customer Service   106

第五部分 单元小结 **Unit Summary**   107

第十单元 运营数据分析 Unit 10 Operational Data Analysis   109

第一部分 课文 **Texts**   110

  一、热身 Warm-up   110
  二、课文 Texts   111
  三、视听说 Viewing, Listening and Speaking   114
  四、学以致用 Practicing What You Have Learnt   115
  五、小知识 Tips   116

第二部分 汉字 **Chinese Characters**   117

  一、汉字知识 Knowledge about Chinese Characters   117

   1. 汉字的笔画（总表） Strokes of Chinese characters (general table)
   2. 汉字的笔顺（总表） Stroke orders of Chinese characters (general table)
   3. 汉字的结构（总表） Structures of Chinese characters (general table)

  二、汉字认读与书写 The Recognition and Writing of Chinese Characters   118

第三部分 日常用语 **Daily Expressions**   118

第四部分 单元实训 **Unit Practical Training**   118

  电商平台运营数据分析 Operational Data Analysis of E-commerce Platforms   118

第五部分 单元小结 **Unit Summary**   119

附录 Appendices   119

词语总表 Vocabulary   121
视频脚本 Video Scripts   131
参考答案 Reference Answers   136

1

Xiāpí chǔfá guīzé
虾皮处罚规则
Punishment Rules of Shopee

Xiāpí chǔfá guīzé
虾皮处罚规则
Punishment Rules of Shopee

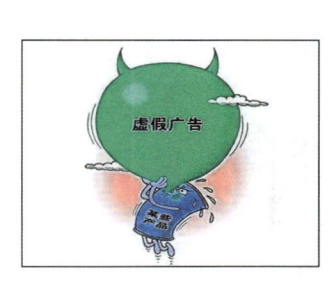

xūjiǎ xiāoshòu
虚假 销售
Wash Sale

bú qiàdàng
不恰当
de guānjiànzì
的关键字
Inappropriate Keywords

bù shí de dìngjià
不实的定价
Deceitful Pricing

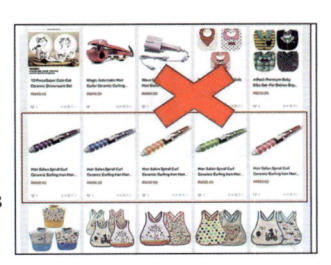

shàngjià
上架
chóngfù shāngpǐn
重复 商品
Listing Duplicated Goods

qīnquán fēngxiǎn
侵权 风险
Risk of Infringement

wèi rènzhèng de
未认证 的
dì-sān fāng ruǎnjiàn
第三方 软件
Uncertified Third-party Software

jìn mài shāngpǐn
禁卖 商品
Prohibited Goods

rǔmà mǎijiā
辱骂买家
Abusing Buyers

1

中文+电子商务（中级）

题解　Introduction

1. 学习内容：虾皮的处罚规则。
   Learning content: The punishment rules of Shopee.
2. 知识目标：掌握与虾皮的处罚规则相关的关键词，学习汉字的笔画"一""丨""丿""乀"、笔顺"先横后竖、先撇后捺"，学写本单元相关汉字。
   Knowledge objectives: To master the keywords related to the punishment rules of Shopee, learn the strokes "一", "丨", "丿", "乀" and the stroke orders "horizontal strokes before vertical strokes, left-falling strokes before right-falling strokes" of Chinese characters, and write the characters related to this unit.
3. 技能目标：学会规避虾皮的处罚规则。
   Skill objectives: To learn to avoid the punishment rules of Shopee.

第一部分　Part 1

课文　Texts

一、热身　rèshēn　Warm-up

1. 给词语选择对应的图片。　Choose the corresponding pictures for the words.

A.

B.

C.

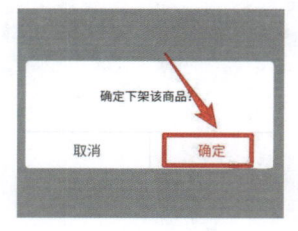

D.

虾皮处罚规则
Punishment Rules of Shopee

dòngjié zhànghù zījīn	shānchú kāndēng shāngpǐn
❶ 冻结 账户 资金 _____	❷ 删除 刊登 商品 _____
freeze account funds	delete published goods
xiànzhì zhànghù quánxiàn	guāntíng diànpù
❸ 限制 账户 权限 _____	❹ 关停 店铺 _____
limit account permissions	close a store

2. 看视频，为对应的处罚原因选择合适的图片。
   Watch the video and choose the appropriate pictures for the corresponding reasons for punishment.

jìnzhǐ zài píngtái mǎimài de huòpǐn
禁止在平台买卖的货品
Goods Prohibited on the Platform

A.　　　　　B.　　　　　C.　　　　　D.

Shòumài qiāngzhī、 dànyào、 jūnhuǒ jí fǎngzhìpǐn.
❶ 售卖 枪支、弹药、军火 及 仿制品。（　）
Selling guns, ammunition, munitions and imitations

Xūjiǎ chǎnpǐn píngjià.
❷ 虚假 产品 评价。（　）
Fake product reviews

Shòumài yòngyú fēifǎ shèxiàng、 lùyīn、 qǔzhèng děng yòngtú de shèbèi.
❸ 售卖 用于 非法 摄像、录音、取证 等 用途 的 设备。（　）
Selling equipment used for illegal video shooting, recording, collection of evidence, etc.

Shòumài guójiā bǎohù lèi zhíwù huótǐ.
❹ 售卖 国家 保护 类 植物 活体。（　）
Selling living plants under national protection

中文＋电子商务（中级）

二、课文 kèwén Texts

A 🎧 01-01

Xiāpí píngtái guān diàn ànlì: Mǎijiā bàomíng cānjiā cùxiāo huódòng, màijiā què yīn
虾皮平台 关店 案例：买家 报名 参加 促销 活动，卖家却因

zìjǐ de yuányīn qǔxiāole dàliàng dìngdān, zàochéng mǎijiā de fùmiàn tǐyàn. Mǎijiā de fǎnkuì
自己的 原因 取消了 大量 订单，造成 买家的 负面 体验。买家的反馈

yǐngxiǎngle píngtái shēngyù, màijiā bìng méiyǒu yǔ píngtái bàobèi liánxì.
影响了 平台 声誉，卖家并 没有与 平台 报备联系。

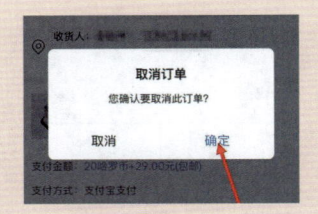

译文 yìwén Text in English

Case of closing stores by Shopee platform: the buyers signed up for promotional activities, but a large number of orders were canceled due to the seller's own reasons, resulting in the buyers' negative experience. The buyers' feedback affected the reputation of the platform, and the seller did not report to or contact the platform.

普通词语 pǔtōng cíyǔ General Vocabulary 🎧 01-02

1.	报名	bàomíng	v.	sign up
2.	参加	cānjiā	v.	join, take part in
3.	却	què	adv.	yet
4.	因	yīn	prep.	because of
5.	自己	zìjǐ	pron.	one's own, oneself
6.	原因	yuányīn	n.	reason
7.	取消	qǔxiāo	v.	cancel
8.	大量	dàliàng	adj.	many, much
9.	造成	zàochéng	v.	result in
10.	影响	yǐngxiǎng	v.	affect
11.	并	bìng	adv.	also
12.	与	yǔ	prep.	with
13.	联系	liánxì	v.	contact

虾皮处罚规则
Punishment Rules of Shopee

专业词语 zhuānyè cíyǔ Specialized Vocabulary 🎧 01-03

1.	关店	guān diàn	phr.	close a store
2.	案例	ànlì	n.	case
3.	买家	mǎijiā	n.	buyer
4.	促销	cùxiāo	v.	promote sales
5.	活动	huódòng	n.	activity
6.	负面	fùmiàn	adj.	negative
7.	体验	tǐyàn	n.	experience
8.	反馈	fǎnkuì	v.	feedback
9.	声誉	shēngyù	n.	reputation
10.	报备	bàobèi	v.	report

B 🎧 01-04

Xiāpí píngtái jiàngdī diànpù quánxiàn ànlì: Màijiā zài diànpù yùnyíng guòchéng zhōng
虾皮平台 降低 店铺 权限 案例：卖家 在 店铺 运营 过程 中

èyì shuādān, jí duō cì wèi chǎnpǐn shuā píngjià、shuā xiāoliàng, bèi píngtái chǔ yǐ jiàngdī
恶意 刷单，即 多 次 为 产品 刷 评价、刷 销量，被 平台 处 以 降低

diànpù quánxiàn děng chéngfá.
店铺 权限 等 惩罚。

译文 yìwén Text in English

Case of downgrading store permissions by Shopee platform: during the store operation process, due to the seller's malicious click farming, which is posting fake reviews and brushing repeatedly for products, the seller is punished by the platform, such as downgrading the store permissions.

普通词语 pǔtōng cíyǔ General Vocabulary 🎧 01-05

1.	降低	jiàngdī	v.	lower
2.	过程	guòchéng	n.	process
3.	中	zhōng	n.	inside, being within a certain range/sphere
4.	多次	duō cì	phr.	many times

| 5. | 被 | bèi | prep. | used in a passive sentence to introduce the agent/doer |
| 6. | 处以 | chǔ yǐ | phr. | be punished by |

专业词语 zhuānyè cíyǔ Specialized Vocabulary 🎧 01-06

1.	店铺权限	diànpù quánxiàn	phr.	store permission
	权限	quánxiàn	n.	permission
2.	恶意	èyì	n.	malice
3.	刷单	shuādān	v.	click farming
	刷	shuā	v.	brush
4.	评价	píngjià	n.	comment, review
5.	销量	xiāoliàng	n.	sales volume
6.	惩罚	chéngfá	v.	punish

三、视听说 shì-tīng-shuō Viewing, Listening and Speaking

1. 看视频，了解电商平台有哪些处罚规则，为相关视频选择正确的选项。
Watch the videos to learn about the punishment rules of e-commerce platforms, and choose the right options for the related videos.

了解 电商 处罚 规则
liǎojiě diànshāng chǔfá guīzé
Learn About Punishment Rules of E-commerce

A. 侵权 风险
qīnquán fēngxiǎn
risk of infringement

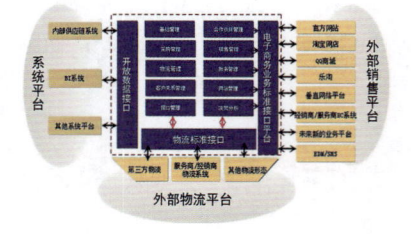

B. 未认证的 第三方 软件
wèi rènzhèng de dì-sān fāng ruǎnjiàn
uncertified third-party software

虾皮处罚规则 **1**
Punishment Rules of Shopee

jìn mài shāngpǐn
C. 禁卖商品
prohibited goods

rǔmà mǎijiā
D. 辱骂买家
abusing buyers

❶ ▶ (　　)　　❷ ▶ (　　)　　❸ ▶ (　　)　　❹ ▶ (　　)

2. 说一说　**Let's talk**

模仿说出电商平台的处罚规则。　**Name the punishment rules of e-commerce platforms following the video.**

四、学以致用　xuéyǐzhìyòng　**Practicing What You Have Learnt**

看视频，学习虾皮平台的处罚规则，判断这些店家违反了什么规则。
Watch the videos to learn the punishment rules of Shopee platform, and judge what punishment rules these stores have violated.

guānyú chǔfá guīzé de ànlì
关于处罚规则的案例
Cases Related to Punishment Rules

xūjiǎ xiāoshòu
A. 虚假销售
wash sale

bú qiàdàng de guānjiànzì
B. 不恰当的关键字
inappropriate keywords

7

bù shí de dìngjià
C. 不实的 定价
deceitful pricing

shàngjià chóngfù shāngpǐn
D. 上架 重复 商品
listing duplicated goods

① ▶ 店家 A（　　　）　　② ▶ 店家 B（　　　）

③ ▶ 店家 C（　　　）　　④ ▶ 店家 D（　　　）

五、小知识　xiǎo zhīshi　Tips

Màijiā jì fēn xìtǒng
卖家计分系统

Xiāpí huì tōngguò màijiā jì fēn xìtǒng guǎnlǐ màijiā bìng jǐyǔ jiǎngchéng, yǐ gǔlì
虾皮会通过卖家计分系统管理卖家并给予奖惩，以鼓励
liánghǎo de màijiā xíngwéi. Mùqián, Xiāpí huì jìsuàn dìngdān wèi wánchéng lǜ、 yánchí
良好的卖家行为。目前，虾皮会计算订单未完成率、延迟
chūhuò lǜ、 wéifǎn shàngjià guīfàn、 lànyòng xíngwéi、 màichǎng kèhù fúwù děng wǔ gè
出货率、违反上架规范、滥用行为、卖场客户服务等五个
xiàngmù. Rú màijiā wèi dádào mùbiāo, píngtái jí huì jǐyǔ kòu fēn chéngfá.
项目。如卖家未达到目标，平台即会给予扣分惩罚。

Seller Rating System

Shopee manages, rewards and punishes the sellers through the seller rating system to encourage good seller behavior. At present, Shopee scores five items: non-fulfilled order rate, late shipped order rate, violation of listing specification, abusive behavior, and store customer service. If the sellers fail to reach the target, the platform will deduct the points.

补充专业词语　bǔchōng zhuānyè cíyǔ　Supplementary Specialized Vocabulary　01-07

1.	冻结账户资金	dòngjié zhànghù zījīn	phr.	freeze account funds
2.	删除刊登商品	shānchú kāndēng shāngpǐn	phr.	delete published goods

3.	限制账户权限	xiànzhì zhànghù quánxiàn	phr.	limit account permissions
4.	关停店铺	guān tíng diànpù	phr.	close a store
5.	虚假产品	xūjiǎ chǎnpǐn	phr.	fake product
6.	非法	fēifǎ	adj.	illegal
7.	侵权风险	qīnquán fēngxiǎn	phr.	risk of infringement
	侵权	qīnquán	v.	infringe on sb.'s rights
8.	辱骂买家	rǔmà mǎijiā	phr.	abuse buyers
9.	禁卖商品	jìn mài shāngpǐn	phr.	prohibited goods
10.	不实定价	bù shí dìngjià	phr.	deceitful pricing

第二部分 Part 2 汉字 Chinese Characters

一、汉字知识 Hànzì zhīshi Knowledge about Chinese Characters

1. 汉字的笔画（1） Strokes of Chinese characters (1)

笔画 Strokes	名称 Names	例字 Examples
一	横 héng	二
丨	竖 shù	十
丿	撇 piě	人
丶	捺 nà	八

2. 汉字的笔顺（1） Stroke orders of Chinese characters (1)

规则 Rules	例字 Examples	笔顺 Stroke orders
先横后竖 Horizontal strokes before vertical strokes	十	一 十
先撇后捺 Left-falling strokes before right-falling strokes	人 八	丿 人 丿 八

二、汉字认读与书写　Hànzì rèndú yǔ shūxiě　The Recognition and Writing of Chinese Characters

认读下列词语，并试着读写构成词语的汉字。
Recognize the following words, and try to read and write the Chinese characters forming these words.

店铺权限　　负面体验　　平台声誉

店			铺			权			限		
负			面			体			验		
平			台			声			誉		

第三部分　Part 3　日常用语　Daily Expressions

① 劳驾，帮我叫辆出租车。Láojià, bāng wǒ jiào liàng chūzūchē. Excuse me, please get me a taxi.
② 明天见。Míngtiān jiàn. See you tomorrow.
③ 不见不散。Bújiàn-búsàn. Be there or be square.

第四部分　Part 4　单元实训　Unit Practical Training

电商平台处罚规则案例分析　diànshāng píngtái chǔfá guīzé ànlì fēnxī
Case Analysis of Punishment Rules of E-commerce Platforms

实训目的 Training purpose

能够了解并规避电商平台的处罚规则。
To be able to learn about and avoid the punishment rules of e-commerce platforms.

实训组织 Training organization

每组三人，设定一个组长。
Three students in each group, with a group leader.

实训内容 Training content

① 学习电商平台的处罚规则。
　 Learn punishment rules of e-commerce platforms.
（1）售卖假货或者有侵权风险的商品；
　　 Selling fake goods or goods with risk of infringement.
（2）使用未认证的第三方软件，并且在短时间内就上传了大量商品。
　　 Using uncertified third-party software and uploading a large number of goods within a short period of time.

（3）辱骂买家或者对买家有过激的语言。
Abusing buyers or using offensive language towards buyers.

（4）售卖平台明文规定的禁卖商品以及限制商品。
Selling prohibited and restricted goods that are expressly stipulated by the platforms.

（5）有不实的售卖行为（虚假销售）。
There are false selling behaviors (wash sale).

（6）设定不恰当的关键字。
Setting inappropriate keywords.

（7）误导及不实的定价。
Misleading and deceitful pricing.

（8）上架重复商品。
Listing duplicated goods.

（9）刷单，刷评价。
Click farming, and posting fake reviews.

❷ 到虾皮平台上去找店铺里有没有相对应的违规案例，讨论这些行为违反了平台的哪一条规则。
Log on to Shopee platform to see if there are corresponding violation cases among the stores, and discuss which rule of the platform these behaviors have violated.

❸ 班级内比赛，看哪一组找到的违规案例最多。
Compete within the class to see which group finds the most violation cases.

❹ 教师点评。
The teacher comments.

第五部分　Part 5
单元小结　Unit Summary

cíyǔ 词语 Vocabulary

普通词语　General Vocabulary

1.	报名	bàomíng	v.	sign up
2.	参加	cānjiā	v.	join, take part in
3.	却	què	adv.	yet
4.	因	yīn	prep.	because of
5.	自己	zìjǐ	pron.	one's own, oneself
6.	原因	yuányīn	n.	reason
7.	取消	qǔxiāo	v.	cancel
8.	大量	dàliàng	adj.	many, much
9.	造成	zàochéng	v.	result in
10.	影响	yǐngxiǎng	v.	affect

词语 cíyǔ Vocabulary

11.	并	bìng	adv.	also
12.	与	yǔ	prep.	with
13.	联系	liánxì	v.	contact
14.	降低	jiàngdī	v.	lower
15.	过程	guòchéng	n.	process
16.	中	zhōng	n.	inside, being within a certain range/sphere
17.	多次	duō cì	phr.	many times
18.	被	bèi	prep.	*used in a passive sentence to introduce the agent/doer*
19.	处以	chǔ yǐ	phr.	be punished by

专业词语 Specialized Vocabulary

1.	关店	guān diàn	phr.	close a store
2.	案例	ànlì	n.	case
3.	买家	mǎijiā	n.	buyer
4.	促销	cùxiāo	v.	promote sales
5.	活动	huódòng	n.	activity
6.	负面	fùmiàn	adj.	negative
7.	体验	tǐyàn	n.	experience
8.	反馈	fǎnkuì	v.	feedback
9.	声誉	shēngyù	n.	reputation
10.	报备	bàobèi	v.	report
11.	店铺权限	diànpù quánxiàn	phr.	store permission
	权限	quánxiàn	n.	permission
12.	恶意	èyì	n.	malice
13.	刷单	shuādān	v.	click farming
	刷	shuā	v.	brush
14.	评价	píngjià	n.	comment, review
15.	销量	xiāoliàng	n.	sales volume
16.	惩罚	chéngfá	v.	punish

虾皮处罚规则
Punishment Rules of Shopee

补充专业词语　Supplementary Specialized Vocabulary

cíyǔ 词语 Vocabulary

1.	冻结账户资金	dòngjié zhànghù zījīn	phr.	freeze account funds
2.	删除刊登商品	shānchú kāndēng shāngpǐn	phr.	delete published goods
3.	限制账户权限	xiànzhì zhànghù quánxiàn	phr.	limit account permissions
4.	关停店铺	guān tíng diànpù	phr.	close a store
5.	虚假产品	xūjiǎ chǎnpǐn	phr.	fake product
6.	非法	fēifǎ	adj.	illegal
7.	侵权风险	qīnquán fēngxiǎn	phr.	risk of infringement
	侵权	qīnquán	v.	infringe on sb.'s rights
8.	辱骂买家	rǔmà mǎijiā	phr.	abuse buyers
9.	禁卖商品	jìn mài shāngpǐn	phr.	prohibited goods
10.	不实定价	bù shí dìngjià	phr.	deceitful pricing

jùzi 句子 Sentences

1. 售卖假货或者有侵权风险的商品。
2. 使用未认证的第三方软件，并且在短时间内就上传了大量商品。
3. 辱骂买家或者对买家有过激的语言。
4. 售卖平台明文规定的禁卖商品以及限制商品。
5. 有不实的售卖行为（虚假销售）。
6. 设定不恰当的关键字。
7. 误导及不实的定价。
8. 上架重复商品。
9. 刷单，刷评价。

2

Jīlì zhèngcè
激励政策
Incentive Policies

jīlì zhèngcè
激励 政策
Incentive Policies

miǎn diànpù yòngjīn
免 店铺 佣金
Free of Commission

cānjiā bāoyóu
参加 包邮
huódòng
活动
Participating in Free Shipping Program

tígōng zīyuánwèi
提供 资源位
Providing Resource-niche

tuīguǎng fèiyong
推广 费用
fǎnxiàn
返现
Cashback of Promotion Expenses

xiànshí tèmài
限时 特卖
Limited Time Offer

xiǎngyǒu yùnfèi
享有 运费
bǔtiē
补贴
Enjoying Freight Allowance

chéngwéi yōuxuǎn
成为 优选
màijiā
卖家
Becoming a Preferred Seller

15

中文＋电子商务（中级）

> **题解　Introduction**
>
> 1. 学习内容：虾皮的激励政策。
>   Learning content: The incentive policies of Shopee.
> 2. 知识目标：掌握与虾皮的激励政策相关的关键词，学习汉字的笔画"、""㇆""㇄""㇂"、笔顺"先上后下、先左后右"，学写本单元相关汉字。
>   Knowledge objectives: To master the keywords related to the incentive policies of Shopee, learn the strokes "、", "㇆", "㇄", "㇂" and the stroke orders "upper strokes before lower strokes, left-side strokes before right-side strokes" of Chinese characters, and write the characters related to this unit.
> 3. 技能目标：学会使用虾皮的激励政策。
>   Skill objectives: To learn to use the incentive policies of Shopee.

第一部分　Part 1

课文　Texts

一、热身　rèshēn　Warm-up

1. 给词语选择对应的图片。　Choose the corresponding pictures for the words.

A.

B.

C.

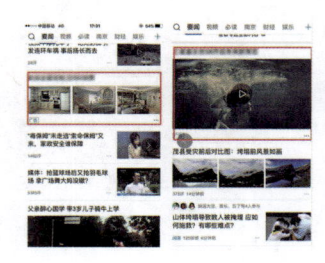

D.

16

激励政策 **2**
Incentive Policies

① miǎn yòngjīn
免 佣金 _____
free of commission

② bāoyóu huódòng
包邮 活动 _____
free shipping program

③ zīyuánwèi
资源位 _____
resource-niche

④ chōngzhí fǎnxiàn
充值 返现 _____
top-up cashback

2. 看视频，选出属于电商平台激励政策的视频。
Watch the videos to select videos that fall under the incentive policies of e-commerce platforms.

xuǎnchū shǔyú diànshāng píngtái jīlì zhèngcè de shìpín
选出 属于 电商 平台 激励 政策 的 视频
Select Videos that Fall Under the Incentive Policies of E-commerce Platforms

① ▶   ② ▶   ③ ▶   ④ ▶

Diànshāng píngtái jīlì zhèngcè bāokuò:
电 商 平台 激励 政策 包括：（　　）
Incentive policies of e-commerce platforms include:

二、课文　kèwén　Texts

A 🎧 02-01

Xiāpí wèile gèng hǎo de tuīdòng lèimù de zēngzhǎng、jiǎnglì biǎoxiàn hǎo de shāngjiā,
虾皮为了更 好地推动 类目的 增长、奖励 表现 好的 商家，

tuīchūle xǔduō zhǒng jīlì zhèngcè, qízhōng bāokuò miǎn diànpù yòngjīn、cānjiā bāoyóu
推出了许多 种 激励 政策，其中 包括 免店铺 佣金、参加包邮

huódòng、tígōng zīyuánwèi、tuīguǎng fèiyong fǎnxiàn děng.
活动、提供 资源位、推广 费用 返现 等。

17

中文 + 电子商务（中级）

译文 yìwén Text in English

In order to better promote the increase in category and reward well-behaved sellers, Shopee has introduced a number of incentive policies, including free of commission, participating in free shipping program, provision of resource-niche, and cashback of promotion expenses.

普通词语 pǔtōng cíyǔ General Vocabulary 02-02

1.	为了	wèile	prep.	for the sake of, in order to
2.	更	gèng	adv.	more
3.	地	de	part.	used after an adjective/a phrase to form an adverbial adjunct before the verb
4.	推动	tuīdòng	v.	promote, push forward
5.	增长	zēngzhǎng	v.	increase
6.	奖励	jiǎnglì	v.	reward
7.	表现	biǎoxiàn	v.	display, manifest
8.	推出	tuīchū	v.	release
9.	许多	xǔduō	num.	many, much
10.	种	zhǒng	m.	kind, type
11.	政策	zhèngcè	n.	policy
12.	其中	qízhōng	n.	among
13.	免	miǎn	v.	exempt

专业词语 zhuānyè cíyǔ Specialized Vocabulary 02-03

1.	商家	shāngjiā	n.	business firm/company/person
2.	激励	jīlì	v.	encourage
3.	佣金	yòngjīn	n.	commission
4.	包邮	bāoyóu	v.	ship for free
5.	资源位	zīyuánwèi	n.	resource-niche
6.	推广	tuīguǎng	v.	promote
7.	费用	fèiyong	n.	expense
8.	返现	fǎnxiàn	v.	cashback

B 02-04

Diànshāng píngtái duì diànpù tígōng jīlì zhèngcè ànlì: Mǒu diànpù yí gè yuè nèi zài
电商 平台对店铺提供激励 政策 案例：某 店铺一个月内在

shíshàng pèishì lèimù zǒnggòng shàng xīn dádào 100 gè, diànpù píngfēn dádào 4.2 fēn.
时尚 配饰 类目 总共 上 新达到100个，店铺 评分 达到4.2分。

Cǐ diànpù huòdéle cānjiā xiànshí tèmài、xiǎngyǒu yùnfèi bǔtiē、chéngwéi yōuxuǎn màijiā de jīhuì.

此店铺 获得了参加限时特卖、享有 运费补贴、成为 优选 卖家 的 机会。

Shopee优选卖家
Preferred Seller

译文 yìwén Text in English

There is a case of e-commerce platforms providing incentive policies to stores: a store has launched 100 new products in the category of fashion accessories in a month, and the store rating reached 4.2 points. This store gets the opportunity to participate in limited time offer, enjoy freight allowance and become a preferred seller.

普通词语 pǔtōng cíyǔ General Vocabulary   02-05

1.	某	mǒu	pron.	some, certain
2.	月	yuè	n.	month
3.	内	nèi	n.	within
4.	时尚	shíshàng	n.	fashion
5.	配饰	pèishì	n.	accessory
6.	总共	zǒnggòng	adv.	altogether, in total
7.	达到	dádào	v.	reach
8.	评分	píngfēn	n.	grade, mark, score
9.	分	fēn	n.	point
10.	此	cǐ	pron.	this
11.	获得	huòdé	v.	get
12.	享有	xiǎngyǒu	v.	enjoy (rights/fame/prestige)
13.	成为	chéngwéi	v.	become
14.	机会	jīhuì	n.	opportunity

专业词语 zhuānyè cíyǔ Specialized Vocabulary   02-06

1.	上新	shàng xīn	phr.	launch something new
2.	限时	xiànshí	v.	limit the time

19

3.	特卖	tèmài	v.	sell at a special discount
4.	运费	yùnfèi	n.	freight
5.	补贴	bǔtiē	n.	subsidy
6.	优选	yōuxuǎn	v.	optimize

三、视听说　shì-tīng-shuō　Viewing, Listening and Speaking

1. 看视频，了解电商卖家激励政策的条件，为相关视频选择正确的选项。
Watch the videos to learn about the conditions of incentive policies for e-commerce sellers, and choose the right options for the related videos.

电商 卖家激励政策的条件
Conditions of Incentive Policies for E-commerce Sellers

A. 当月 上 新 数量 达到 200
dàngyuè shàng xīn shùliàng dádào 200
volume of the new arrivals in the month reaches 200

B. 当月 上 新 数量 达到 100
dàngyuè shàng xīn shùliàng dádào 100
volume of the new arrivals in the month reaches 100

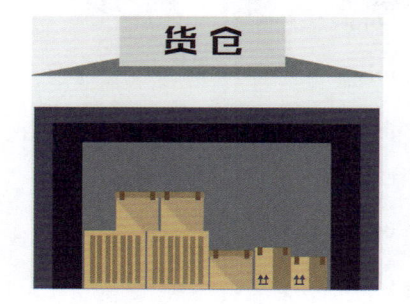

C. 目标类目 上 新达到 200
mùbiāo lèimù shàng xīn dádào 200
the new arrivals in the target category reach 200

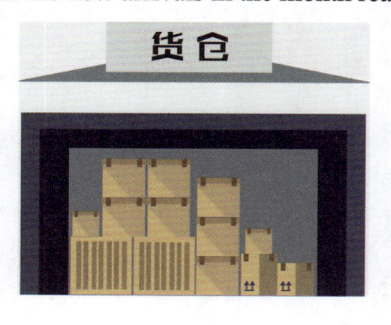

D. 目标类目 上 新达到 300
mùbiāo lèimù shàng xīn dádào 300
the new arrivals in the target category reach 300

① ▶ (　)　② ▶ (　)　③ ▶ (　)　④ ▶ (　)

2.说一说　Let's talk

模仿说出电商卖家激励政策的条件。　Name the conditions of incentive policies for e-commerce sellers following the videos.

四、学以致用　xuéyǐzhìyòng　Practicing What You Have Learnt

看视频，学习虾皮平台激励政策的等级，判断这些卖家可以获得哪个等级的激励政策。
Watch the video to learn the levels of incentive policies of Shopee platform and judge which level of incentive policies these sellers can obtain.

Xiāpí píngtái jīlì zhèngcè de děngjí
虾皮平台激励政策的等级
Incentive Policy Levels of Shopee Platform

　　　rùzhù shíjiān zài liǎng dào sān gè yuè de màijiā
A. 入驻时间在两到三个月的卖家
　　sellers who have entered for two to three months

　　diànpù píngfēn dádào 4.2 fēn yǐshàng
B. 店铺评分达到4.2分以上
　　the store rating is above 4.2 points

　　diànpù zài kāi diàn yí gè yuè nèi shàng xīn shùliàng
C. 店铺在开店一个月内上新数量
　　dádào 50
　　达到50
　　the store has launched 50 new products within the first month

　　xīn diàn shàng xīn chǎnpǐn fúhé mùbiāo jiàgé
D. 新店上新产品符合目标价格
　　yāoqiú
　　要求
　　the newly launched products of a new store have met the target price requirements

21

❶ Huòdé xīn màijiā děngjí jīlì zhèngcè de shì:
獲得新卖家等级激励政策 的是:( )

The ones who obtain the new seller level of incentive polices are:

❷ Huòdé fēi xīn màijiā děngjí jīlì zhèngcè de shì:
获得非新卖家等级激励政策 的是:( )

The ones who obtain the non-new seller level of incentive policies are:

五、小知识 xiǎo zhīshi Tips

如何 成为 优选 卖家
Rúhé chéngwéi yōuxuǎn màijiā

优选卖家是指 商品 受 欢迎、提供良好 服务、得到买家一致 好评 的卖家。成为 优选卖家的 标准：店铺 评分达到 4.8 分 以上，店铺当季累计惩罚积分为0分，订单未 完成 率小于10%，店内 没有任何盗版 或者 侵权 产品。

How to Become a Preferred Seller

A preferred seller refers to a seller that offers popular products and good service, and receives unanimous praise from the buyers. The criteria to be a preferred seller are: the store rating is above 4.8 points, the cumulative punishment points of the store in the current season are 0, non-fulfilled order rate <10%, and there are no pirated or infringing products in the store.

补充专业词语 bǔchōng zhuānyè cíyǔ Supplementary Specialized Vocabulary   🎧 02-07

1.	充值	chōngzhí	v.	top up
2.	库存	kùcún	n.	stock
3.	盗版	dàobǎn	n.	pirated edition
4.	价格段	jiàgé duàn	phr.	price tier

激励政策 2
Incentive Policies

第二部分 Part 2
汉字 Chinese Characters

一、汉字知识　Hànzì zhīshi　Knowledge about Chinese Characters

1. 汉字的笔画（2）　Strokes of Chinese characters (2)

笔画 Strokes	名称 Names	例字 Examples
丶	点 diǎn	六
𠃍	横折 héngzhé	口、日、五
ㄴ	竖折 shùzhé	山
ㄥ	撇折 piězhé	么

2. 汉字的笔顺（2）　Stroke orders of Chinese characters (2)

规则 Rules	例字 Examples	笔顺 Stroke orders
先上后下 Upper strokes before lower strokes	三	一 二 三
先左后右 Left-side strokes before right-side strokes	人	丿 人

二、汉字认读与书写　Hànzì rèndú yǔ shūxiě　The Recognition and Writing of Chinese Characters

认读下列词语，并试着读写构成词语的汉字。
Recognize the following words, and try to read and write the Chinese characters forming these words.

店铺评分　　限时特卖　　运费补贴

店			铺			评			分		
限			时			特			卖		
运			费			补			贴		

第三部分 Part 3
日常用语 Daily Expressions

❶ 最近怎么样？　Zuìjìn zěnmeyàng? How are you doing these days?
❷ 认识您很高兴。　Rènshi nín hěn gāoxìng. Nice to meet you.

23

第四部分 Part 4　单元实训 Unit Practical Training

电商平台激励政策案例分析　diànshāng píngtái jīlì zhèngcè ànlì fēnxī
Case Analysis of Incentive Policies of E-commerce Platforms

实训目的 Training purpose
了解并能有效利用电商平台的激励政策。
To learn about incentive policies of e-commerce platforms, and be able to make effective use of them.

实训组织 Training organization
每组三人，设定一个组长。
Three students in each group, with a group leader.

实训内容 Training content
❶ 学习电商平台的激励政策。

　　Learn incentive policies of e-commerce platforms.

（1）达标店铺在下月享受包邮活动奖励。

　　The stores meeting the standards enjoy free shipping next month.

（2）特定商品获得优先推广。

　　Specific products are given priority in promotion.

（3）获得付费广告充值一次。

　　Get paid advertising top up once.

（4）平台免费直播推广两次。

　　Free live promotion on the platform twice.

（5）为店铺免费宣传一次。

　　Free promotion for the store once.

❷ 到虾皮平台上寻找店铺里有没有相对应的奖励政策，讨论这些店铺的达标条件。

　　Log on to Shopee platform to see if there are corresponding reward polices in the stores, and discuss the conditions for these stores to meet the standards.

❸ 班级内比赛，看哪一组找到的激励政策的案例最多。

　　Compete within the class to see which group finds the most cases with incentive policies.

❹ 教师点评。

　　 The teacher comments.

第五部分　Part 5

单元小结 Unit Summary

词语 / cíyǔ / Vocabulary

普通词语　General Vocabulary

1.	为了	wèile	prep.	for the sake of, in order to
2.	更	gèng	adv.	more
3.	地	de	part.	*used after an adjective/a phrase to form an adverbial adjunct before the verb*
4.	推动	tuīdòng	v.	promote, push forward
5.	增长	zēngzhǎng	v.	increase
6.	奖励	jiǎnglì	v.	reward
7.	表现	biǎoxiàn	v.	display, manifest
8.	推出	tuīchū	v.	release
9.	许多	xǔduō	num.	many, much
10.	种	zhǒng	m.	kind, type
11.	政策	zhèngcè	n.	policy
12.	其中	qízhōng	n.	among
13.	免	miǎn	v.	exempt
14.	某	mǒu	pron.	some, certain
15.	月	yuè	n.	month
16.	内	nèi	n.	within
17.	时尚	shíshàng	n.	fashion
18.	配饰	pèishì	n.	accessory
19.	总共	zǒnggòng	adv.	altogether, in total
20.	达到	dádào	v.	reach
21.	评分	píngfēn	n.	grade, mark, score
22.	分	fēn	n.	point
23.	此	cǐ	pron.	this
24.	获得	huòdé	v.	get
25.	享有	xiǎngyǒu	v.	enjoy (rights/fame/prestige)
26.	成为	chéngwéi	v.	become
27.	机会	jīhuì	n.	opportunity

激励政策　2　Incentive Policies

25

专业词语　Specialized Vocabulary

1.	商家	shāngjiā	n.	business firm/company/person
2.	激励	jīlì	v.	encourage
3.	佣金	yòngjīn	n.	commission
4.	包邮	bāoyóu	v.	ship for free
5.	资源位	zīyuánwèi	n.	resource-niche
6.	推广	tuīguǎng	v.	promote
7.	费用	fèiyong	n.	expense
8.	返现	fǎnxiàn	v.	cashback
9.	上新	shàng xīn	phr.	launch something new
10.	限时	xiànshí	v.	limit the time
11.	特卖	tèmài	v.	sell at a special discount
12.	运费	yùnfèi	n.	freight
13.	补贴	bǔtiē	n.	subsidy
14.	优选	yōuxuǎn	v.	optimize

补充专业词语　Supplementary Specialized Vocabulary

1.	充值	chōngzhí	v.	top up
2.	库存	kùcún	n.	stock
3.	盗版	dàobǎn	n.	pirated edition
4.	价格段	jiàgé duàn	phr.	price tier

cíyǔ 词语 Vocabulary

jùzi 句子 Sentences

1. 电商平台推出了许多种激励政策。
2. 电商平台有免店铺佣金的激励政策。
3. 电商平台有推广费用返现的激励政策。
4. 电商平台还有参加包邮活动和提供资源位的激励政策。
5. 某店铺在一个月内上新数量达到 100 个。
6. 店铺评分达到 4.2 分。
7. 店铺获得参加限时特卖的机会。
8. 店铺获得运费补贴的机会。
9. 店铺获得成为优选卖家的机会。

3

Bàokuǎn dǎzào
爆款打造
The Shaping of Hot-Selling Products

bàokuǎn dǎzào de liúchéng
爆款 打造 的 流程
Process of Shaping Hot-Selling Products

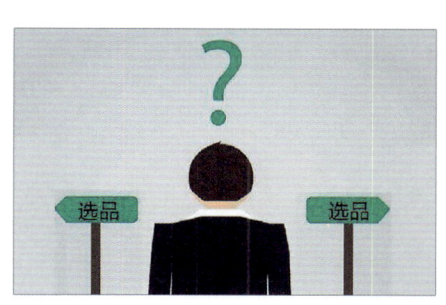

xuǎnzé yǒu màidiǎn de chǎnpǐn
选择 有 卖点 的 产品
Select Products with Selling Points

yōuhuà chǎnpǐn biāotí hé zhǔtú
优化 产品 标题和主图
Optimize Product Titles and Main Images

zhìdìng yǒu xīyǐnlì de jiàgé
制定 有 吸引力 的 价格
Set Attractive Prices

cùxiāo yǔ tuīguǎng
促销 与 推广
Promotion and Advertising

题解 Introduction

1. 学习内容：爆款打造的流程和要点。
   Learning content: The process and key points of the shaping of hot-selling products.
2. 知识目标：掌握与爆款打造相关的关键词，学习汉字的笔画 "㇀" "亅" "丿" "乚"、笔顺 "先中间后两边、先外边后里边"，学写本单元相关汉字。
   Knowledge objectives: To master the keywords related to the shaping of hot-selling products, learn the strokes "㇀", "亅", "丿", "乚" and the stroke orders "strokes in the middle before those on both sides", "outside strokes before inside strokes" of Chinese characters, and write the characters related to this unit.
3. 技能目标：学会进行爆款打造。
   Skill objectives: To learn to shape hot-selling products.

第一部分　Part 1

课文　Texts

一、热身　rèshēn　Warm-up

1. 给词语选择对应的图片。Choose the corresponding pictures for the words.

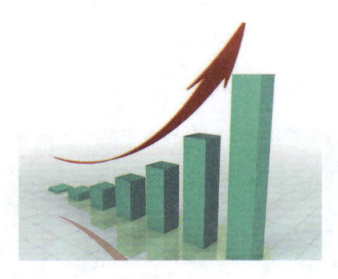

A.

B.

C.

D.

爆款打造
The Shaping of Hot-Selling Products

bàokuǎn	xuǎn pǐn
❶ 爆款 _____	❷ 选品 _____
hot-selling product	product selection

yǐnliú	xiāoliàng zēngzhǎng
❸ 引流 _____	❹ 销量增长 _____
traffic driving	sales volume growth

2. 看视频，了解爆款打造的流程，将下面的步骤排序。

Watch the video to learn about the process of shaping hot-selling products and arrange the following steps in order.

bàokuǎn dǎzào de liúchéng
爆款打造的流程
Process of Shaping Hot-Selling Products

dìngjià
❶ 定价
setting a price

yōuhuà chǎnpǐn biāotí hé zhǔtú
❷ 优化产品标题和主图
optimizing product titles and main images

xuǎnzé héshì de chǎnpǐn
❸ 选择合适的产品
selecting appropriate products

chǎnpǐn de cùxiāo yǔ tuīguǎng
❹ 产品的促销与推广
promoting and advertising products

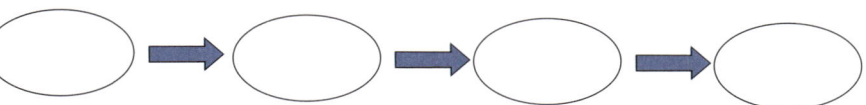

○ → ○ → ○ → ○

29

二、课文 kèwén Texts

A 03-01

Xuǎnzé héshì de chǎnpǐn shì bàokuǎn dǎzào de guānjiàn. Xuǎn pǐn xūyào kǎolǜ diànpù
选择合适的产品是爆款打造的关键。选品需要考虑店铺

dìngwèi、chǎnpǐn jìngzhēnglì、jìjié shǔxìng、dāngdì shìchǎng de xiāofèi xíguàn děng yīnsù.
定位、产品竞争力、季节属性、当地市场的消费习惯等因素。

Zhǐyǒu zhèyàng, cái néng xuǎnchū jùbèi bàokuǎn qiánzhì de chǎnpǐn.
只有这样，才能选出具备爆款潜质的产品。

译文 yìwén Text in English

The selection of appropriate products is the key to shaping hot-selling products. During product selection, the store orientation, product competitiveness, seasonal attribute, consumption habit of the local market and other factors shall be taken into account. Only in this way can potential hot-selling products be selected.

普通词语 pǔtōng cíyǔ General Vocabulary 03-02

1.	合适	héshì	adj.	proper, right
2.	关键	guānjiàn	n.	key
3.	需要	xūyào	v.	need, demand
4.	考虑	kǎolǜ	v.	consider
5.	定位	dìngwèi	n.	orientation, niche
6.	当地	dāngdì	n.	locality
7.	市场	shìchǎng	n.	market
8.	因素	yīnsù	n.	element, factor
9.	只有	zhǐyǒu	conj.	only
10.	这样	zhèyàng	pron.	this way, such
11.	才	cái	adv.	used to indicate that sth. happens only under certain conditions
12.	能	néng	aux.	can
13.	选出	xuǎnchū	phr.	select

爆款打造
The Shaping of Hot-Selling Products

| 14. | 具备 | jùbèi | v. | have |
| 15. | 潜质 | qiánzhì | n. | potential |

专业词语 zhuānyè cíyǔ Specialized Vocabulary 🎧 03-03

1.	产品	chǎnpǐn	n.	product
2.	爆款	bàokuǎn	n.	hot-selling product
3.	打造	dǎzào	v.	shape, make
4.	选品	xuǎn pǐn	phr.	product selection
5.	竞争力	jìngzhēnglì	n.	competitiveness
6.	季节属性	jìjié shǔxìng	phr.	seasonal attribute
7.	消费习惯	xiāofèi xíguàn	phr.	consumption habit

B 🎧 03-04

Dìngjià shì bàokuǎn dǎzào de zhòngyào yīnsù. Jiàgé yào zài tónglèi chǎnpǐn li jùyǒu yōushì, cái néng xīyǐn gùkè. Lìngwài, cānyù píngtái de cùxiāo hé tuīguǎng yě shì diànpù yǐnliú, xiāoliàng zēngzhǎng, bàokuǎn dǎzào bìbùkěshǎo de huánjié.

定价是爆款打造的重要因素。价格要在同类产品里具有优势，才能吸引顾客。另外，参与平台的促销和推广也是店铺引流、销量增长、爆款打造必不可少的环节。

译文 yìwén Text in English

Pricing is an important factor for the shaping of hot-selling products. The price must be advantageous among similar products to attract customers. In addition, participating in sales promotion and advertising of the platform is also an essential step for driving traffic, boosting sales volume and shaping hot-selling products.

普通词语 pǔtōng cíyǔ General Vocabulary 🎧 03-05

1.	重要	zhòngyào	adj.	important
2.	同类	tónglèi	n.	of the same kind/category
3.	具有	jùyǒu	v.	have

4.	优势	yōushì	n.	advantage
5.	吸引	xīyǐn	v.	attract
6.	另外	lìngwài	conj.	besides
7.	参与	cānyù	v.	participate in
8.	必不可少	bìbùkěshǎo	phr.	essential, indispensable
9.	环节	huánjié	n.	link

专业词语 zhuānyè cíyǔ Specialized Vocabulary 🎧 03-06

| 1. | 定价 | dìng//jià | v. | set a price |
| 2. | 引流 | yǐnliú | v. | drive traffic |

三、视听说 shì-tīng-shuō Viewing, Listening & Speaking

1. 看视频，了解选品时需要注意哪些方面，为相关视频选择正确的选项，并模仿说一说如何选品。

Watch the videos to learn what aspects need to be taken care of during product selection. Choose the right options for the related videos, and talk about how to select products following the videos.

xuānzé chǎnpǐn de guānzhù shìxiàng
选择产品的关注事项
Precautions for Product Selection

A. diànpù dìngwèi jí mùbiāo rénqún
店铺定位及目标人群
store orientation and target group

B. shìchǎng fēnxī hé xiāofèi xíguàn
市场分析和消费习惯
market analysis and consumption habit

爆款打造　3
The Shaping of Hot-Selling Products

　　　　jìjié shǔxìng hé liúxíng qūshì　　　　　　　chǎnpǐn zhìliàng jí yōushì
C. 季节属性和流行趋势　　　　　　　D. 产品质量及优势
　　seasonal attribute and fashion trend　　　　　product quality and advantages

① ▶ (　　)　② ▶ (　　)　③ ▶ (　　)　④ ▶ (　　)

2. 说一说　Let's talk

模仿说出爆款打造的流程。　**Name the process of shaping hot-selling products following the videos.**

　　　　四、学以致用　xuéyǐzhìyòng　**Practicing What You Have Learnt**

看视频，了解虾皮平台的促销活动和广告推广，选出新店打造爆款时适合参加的活动及使用的广告。
Watch the video to learn sales promotion and advertising on Shopee platform, and choose appropriate activities to participate in and advertisements to use when shaping hot-selling products for the new store.

　　miǎoshā huódòng　　　　　　pǐnlèi huódòng　　　　　"Shuāng Shíyī" cùxiāo huódòng
A. 秒杀活动　　　　　B. 品类活动　　　　　C. "双十一"促销活动
　　second kill　　　　　　　category campaign　　　　　Double Eleven big sale
　　(　　)　　　　　　　　　(　　)　　　　　　　　　(　　)

33

中文 + 电子商务（中级）

D. 关键词广告 guānjiàncí guǎnggào
keyword advertisements
(   )

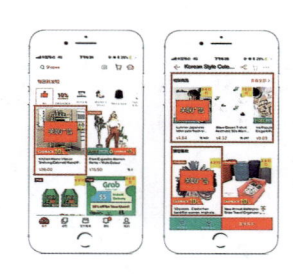

E. 关联广告 guānlián guǎnggào
discovery advertisements
(   )

F. 商店广告 shāngdiàn guǎnggào
store advertisements
(   )

五、小知识 xiǎo zhīshi Tips

流量扶持 Liúliàng fúchí

虾皮平台会给予新店铺免费的流量扶持。店铺可以通过定时定量地上新产品获得免费的流量。前期的上新流量是新店铺获取流量的主要来源。新品的扶持流量可以带动其他产品的流量，从而提升店铺的流量与权重。

Traffic Support

Shopee platform provides free traffic support to new stores. Stores can get free traffic by launching new products regularly in certain quantities. The new product traffic at the early stage is the main source for new stores to obtain traffic, and the supporting traffic of new products can direct traffic to other products, thus improving the traffic and weightiness of the store.

补充专业词语 bǔchōng zhuānyè cíyǔ Supplementary Specialized Vocabulary 03-07

1.	店铺定位	diànpù dìngwèi	phr.	store orientation
2.	目标人群	mùbiāo rénqún	phr.	target group
3.	市场分析	shìchǎng fēnxī	phr.	market analysis
4.	流行趋势	liúxíng qūshì	phr.	fashion trend
5.	秒杀活动	miǎoshā huódòng	phr.	second kill
6.	品类活动	pǐnlèi huódòng	phr.	category campaign
7.	关键词广告	guānjiàncí guǎnggào	phr.	keyword advertisement

	广告	guǎnggào	n.	advertisement
8.	关联广告	guānlián guǎnggào	phr.	discovery advertisement
9.	商店广告	shāngdiàn guǎnggào	phr.	store advertisement

第二部分 Part 2 汉字 Chinese Characters

一、汉字知识 Hànzì zhīshi Knowledge about Chinese Characters

1. 汉字的笔画（3） Strokes of Chinese characters (3)

笔画 Strokes	名称 Names	例字 Examples
㇇	横钩 hénggōu	买
亅	竖钩 shùgōu	小
乚	弯钩 wāngōu	子
ㄥ	竖弯钩 shùwāngōu	七

2. 汉字的笔顺（3） Stroke orders of Chinese characters (3)

规则 Rules	例字 Examples	笔顺 Stroke orders
先中间后两边 Strokes in the middle before those on both sides	小	亅 小 小
先外边后里边 Outside strokes before inside strokes	问	丶 丷 门 问 问 问

二、汉字认读与书写 Hànzì rèndú yǔ shūxiě The Recognition and Writing of Chinese Characters

认读下列词语，并试着读写构成词语的汉字。
Recognize the following words, and try to read and write the Chinese characters forming these words.

爆款打造　竞争力　消费习惯

爆			款			打			造		
竞			争			力			消		
费			习			惯					

第三部分　Part 3　日常用语　Daily Expressions

❶ 我来介绍一下儿，这位是李伟先生。Wǒ lái jièshào yíxiàr, zhè wèi shì Lǐ Wěi xiānsheng. Let me make an introduction. This is Mr. Li Wei.

❷ 请问，南京饭店在哪儿？ Qǐngwèn, Nánjīng Fàndiàn zài nǎr? Excuse me, where's Nanjing Hotel?

第四部分　Part 4　单元实训　Unit Practical Training

店铺爆款打造策划　diànpù bàokuǎn dǎzào cèhuà
Stores' Planning of Shaping Hot-Selling Products

实训目的 Training purpose

熟悉爆款打造的流程，学会策划、打造店铺的爆款产品。

To get familiar with the process of shaping hot-selling products, and learn to plan and shape hot-selling products for the store.

实训组织 Training organization

每组三人，设定一个组长。

Three students in each group, with a group leader.

实训内容 Training content

❶ 小组成员在虾皮平台上选择一家店铺，根据店铺的产品类目、目标市场，结合当前的季节特点以及流行趋势，通过讨论确定一款具有爆款潜质的产品。

The group members select a store on Shopee platform. After discussion, they determine a product with the potential to be hot-selling on the basis of product category and target market of the store, combined with the current seasonal characteristics and fashion trends.

❷ 小组第一位成员负责产品的标题和图片，根据产品详情页的介绍拟定标题，选择最有卖点的图片作为主图。

The first member is responsible for the title and images of the product. Propose a title according to the introduction on the detail page of the product and choose a picture with the best selling point as the main image.

❸ 第二位成员负责定价，参考平台上同类产品的价格，确定一个有竞争力的价格。

The second member is responsible for pricing. Set a competitive price with reference to the prices of similar products on the platform.

❹ 第三位成员负责产品的推广，根据产品的特点，选择合适的平台活动以及广告推广形式。

The third member is responsible for the product promotion. Choose appropriate platform sale campaigns and forms of advertising promotion based on the product characteristics.

❺ 小组形成一个完整的策划方案，向全班展示。
The group forms a complete planning scheme and presents it to the class.

❻ 教师点评。
The teacher comments.

第五部分　Part 5　单元小结　Unit Summary

词语 cíyǔ Vocabulary

普通词语　General Vocabulary

1.	合适	héshì	adj.	proper, right
2.	关键	guānjiàn	n.	key
3.	需要	xūyào	v.	need, demand
4.	考虑	kǎolǜ	v.	consider
5.	定位	dìngwèi	n.	orientation, niche
6.	当地	dāngdì	n.	locality
7.	市场	shìchǎng	n.	market
8.	因素	yīnsù	n.	element, factor
9.	只有	zhǐyǒu	conj.	only
10.	这样	zhèyàng	pron.	this way, such
11.	才	cái	adv.	used to indicate that sth. happens only under certain conditions
12.	能	néng	aux.	can
13.	选出	xuǎnchū	phr.	select
14.	具备	jùbèi	v.	have
15.	潜质	qiánzhì	n.	potential
16.	重要	zhòngyào	adj.	important
17.	同类	tónglèi	n.	of the same kind/category
18.	具有	jùyǒu	v.	have
19.	优势	yōushì	n.	advantage
20.	吸引	xīyǐn	v.	attract
21.	另外	lìngwài	conj.	besides
22.	参与	cānyù	v.	participate in
23.	必不可少	bìbùkěshǎo	phr.	essential, indispensable
24.	环节	huánjié	n.	link

中文 + 电子商务（中级）

词语 cíyǔ Vocabulary

专业词语　Specialized Vocabulary

1.	产品	chǎnpǐn	n.	product
2.	爆款	bàokuǎn	n.	hot-selling product
3.	打造	dǎzào	v.	shape, make
4.	选品	xuǎn pǐn	phr.	product selection
5.	竞争力	jìngzhēnglì	n.	competitiveness
6.	季节属性	jìjié shǔxìng	phr.	seasonal attribute
7.	消费习惯	xiāofèi xíguàn	phr.	consumption habit
8.	定价	dìng//jià	v.	set a price
9.	引流	yǐnliú	v.	drive traffic

补充专业词语　Supplementary Specialized Vocabulary

1.	店铺定位	diànpù dìngwèi	phr.	store orientation
2.	目标人群	mùbiāo rénqún	phr.	target group
3.	市场分析	shìchǎng fēnxī	phr.	market analysis
4.	流行趋势	liúxíng qūshì	phr.	fashion trend
5.	秒杀活动	miǎoshā huódòng	phr.	second kill
6.	品类活动	pǐnlèi huódòng	phr.	category campaign
7.	关键词广告	guānjiàncí guǎnggào	phr.	keyword advertisement
	广告	guǎnggào	n.	advertisement
8.	关联广告	guānlián guǎnggào	phr.	discovery advertisement
9.	商店广告	shāngdiàn guǎnggào	phr.	store advertisement

句子 jùzi Sentences

1. 爆款打造主要包括选品、优化产品标题和主图、定价及促销推广四个环节。
2. 选择合适的产品是爆款打造的关键。
3. 选品需要考虑店铺定位、产品竞争力、季节属性、当地市场的消费习惯等因素。
4. 定价是爆款打造的重要因素。
5. 价格要在同类产品里具有优势，才能吸引顾客。
6. 参与平台的促销和推广也是爆款打造必不可少的环节。

4

Biāotí yōuhuà
标题优化
Title Optimization

biāotí yōuhuà
标题 优化
Title Optimization

yǔ chǎnpǐn gāodù xiāngguān
与产品 高度 相关
Highly Related to the Product

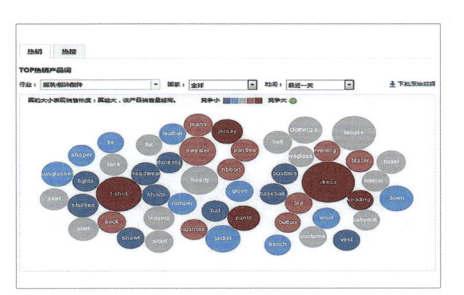

xuǎnzé rèsōucí
选择热搜词
Select the Hot Search Terms

tūchū màidiǎn
突出 卖点
Highlight the Selling Points

jiǎnjié míngliǎo
简洁 明了
Be Concise and Clear

题解　Introduction

1. 学习内容：产品标题优化的目的和方法。
   Learning content: The purpose and methods of product title optimization.
2. 知识目标：掌握与产品标题优化相关的关键词，学习汉字的笔画"㇀""㇂""㇁""乀"、笔顺"先外后里再封口"，学写本单元相关汉字。
   Knowledge objectives: To master the keywords related to product title optimization, learn the strokes "㇀", "㇂", "㇁", "乀" and the stroke order "outside strokes before inside strokes, and then sealing strokes" of Chinese characters, and write the characters related to this unit.
3. 技能目标：学会优化产品标题。
   Skill objectives: To learn to optimize product titles.

第一部分　Part 1

课文　Texts

一、热身　rèshēn　Warm-up

1. 给词语选择对应的图片。　Choose the corresponding pictures for the words.

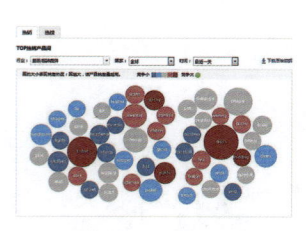

A.

B.

C.

D.

标题优化 4
Title Optimization

① 产品 标题 _____ chǎnpǐn biāotí
product title

② 热搜词 _____ rèsōucí
hot search term

③ 关键词 _____ guānjiàncí
keyword

④ 卖点 _____ màidiǎn
selling point

2. 看视频，了解产品标题，将下面四个标题与所售产品匹配。
Watch the video to learn about product titles and match the four titles below with the products being sold.

A. 手机 shǒujī
cell phone

B. 鞋 xié
shoes

C. 电脑 diànnǎo
computer

D. 包 bāo
bag

① ( )
李宁跑步鞋男鞋2021夏季新款网面透气跑鞋eazGO男士鞋子运动鞋男
领券满300减30

② ( )
华为电脑Matebook X Pro 2021款超薄本13.9英寸全面屏笔记本电脑轻薄商务触屏超极本
下单送无线鼠标，晒单送双肩包，咨询更优惠

③ ( )
Huawei/华为 Mate 20 X华为mate20x手机官方旗舰店5G官网正品全国联保
原装正品 全国联保

④ ( )
爱迪生中学生书包男大容量双肩包小学生初中生高中生减负防水背包
防泼水 轻便减负 顺丰包邮

二、课文 kèwén Texts

A 04-01

Biāotí nénggòu ràng mǎijiā kuàisù liǎojiě chǎnpǐn xìnxī. Hǎo de chǎnpǐn biāotí tōngcháng
标题能够让买家快速了解产品信息。好的产品标题通常
bāokuò pǐnpáimíng、chǎnpǐnmíng、rèsōucí hé màidiǎncí. Rèsōucí juédìngle chǎnpǐn néngfǒu
包括品牌名、产品名、热搜词和卖点词。热搜词决定了产品能否
bèi liúlǎnzhě kàndào, màidiǎncí shì juédìng liúlǎnzhě shìfǒu xiàdān de guānjiàn.
被浏览者看到，卖点词是决定浏览者是否下单的关键。

译文 yìwén Text in English

The title enables the buyers to learn about the product information quickly. A good product title usually includes brand name, product name, hot search terms and selling point terms. The hot search terms decide whether the product can be found by the viewers, while the selling point terms are the key to deciding whether the viewers place an order or not.

普通词语 pǔtōng cíyǔ General Vocabulary 04-02

1.	能够	nénggòu	aux.	can
2.	让	ràng	v.	let
3.	快速	kuàisù	adj.	quick
4.	了解	liǎojiě	v.	learn about, understand
5.	通常	tōngcháng	adv.	usually
6.	名	míng	n.	name
7.	决定	juédìng	v.	decide
8.	能否	néngfǒu	v.	can or cannot
9.	看到	kàndào	phr.	see
10.	是否	shìfǒu	adv.	whether... or not

标题优化
Title Optimization

专业词语 zhuānyè cíyǔ Specialized Vocabulary 🎧 04-03

1.	标题	biāotí	n.	title
2.	热搜词	rèsōucí	n.	hot search term
3.	卖点词	màidiǎncí	n.	selling point term
	卖点	màidiǎn	n.	selling point
4.	浏览者	liúlǎnzhě	n.	viewer

B 🎧 04-04

Biāotí yōuhuà kěyǐ tíshēng chǎnpǐn de sōusuǒ liúliàng hé diǎnjīlǜ. Yōuhuà biāotí shí yào
标题优化可以提升产品的搜索流量和点击率。优化标题时要

zhùyì yǐxià sān diǎn: Dì-yī, biāotí yào jiǎnjié míngliǎo, kědúxìng qiáng; dì-èr, biāotí
注意以下三点：第一，标题要简洁明了，可读性强；第二，标题

yào tūchū màidiǎn hé yōushì; dì-sān, guānjiàncí yào jīngtiāo-xìxuǎn.
要突出卖点和优势；第三，关键词要精挑细选。

译文 yìwén Text in English

Title optimization can increase products' search traffic and click-through rates. When optimizing titles, pay attention to the following three points. First, the title should be concise and clear, and have high readability. Second, the title should highlight the selling points and advantages. Third, the keywords should be carefully selected.

普通词语 pǔtōng cíyǔ General Vocabulary 🎧 04-05

1.	提升	tíshēng	v.	promote
2.	时	shí	n.	a period of time
3.	注意	zhùyì	v.	pay attention to
4.	以下	yǐxià	n.	the following
5.	三	sān	num.	three
6.	点	diǎn	m.	*used in counting items*
7.	第	dì	pref.	*a prefix indicating ordinal numbers*
8.	简洁	jiǎnjié	adj.	concise
9.	明了	míngliǎo	adj.	clear
10.	可读性	kědúxìng	n.	readability

中文+电子商务（中级）

11.	强	qiáng	adj.	strong, resolute
12.	突出	tūchū	v.	lay emphasis on
13.	精挑细选	jīngtiāo-xìxuǎn	phr.	carefully select

专业词语 zhuānyè cíyǔ Specialized Vocabulary 🎧 04-06

1.	优化	yōuhuà	v.	optimize
2.	搜索	sōusuǒ	v.	search
3.	流量	liúliàng	n.	traffic, volume of flow
4.	点击率	diǎnjīlǜ	n.	click-through rate

三、视听说 shì-tīng-shuō   Viewing, Listening and Speaking

1. 看视频，了解关键词优化的技巧，判断下列说法是否正确，并模仿说一说如何选择标题的关键词。
Watch the video to learn about the techniques of keyword optimization, decide whether the following statements are true or false, and talk about how to choose keywords for titles following the video.

（标题优化技巧 / Techniques of Title Optimization）

❶ Guānjiàncí yào yǔ chǎnpǐn gāodù xiāngguān.
关键词 要与产品 高度 相关。（　　）
The keywords should be highly related to the product.

❷ Guānjiàncí bú yào xuǎnzé rèsōucí.
关键词 不要 选择 热搜词。（　　）
Do not select hot search terms as keywords.

❸ Guānjiàncí yào tūchū màidiǎn.
关键词 要突出卖点。（　　）
The keywords should highlight the selling points.

❹ Kěyǐ bǎoliú wúxiào guānjiàncí.
可以保留无效 关键词。（　　）
Invalid keywords can be kept.

标题优化 4
Title Optimization

2. 说一说　Let's talk

模仿说出优化产品标题的方法。　Name ways to optimize product titles following the video.

四、学以致用　xuéyǐzhìyòng　Practicing What You Have Learnt

看视频，了解产品标题的组成部分，在画线的关键词旁填入相应的选项。
Watch the video to learn about the components of a product title and fill in the corresponding options next to the underlined keywords.

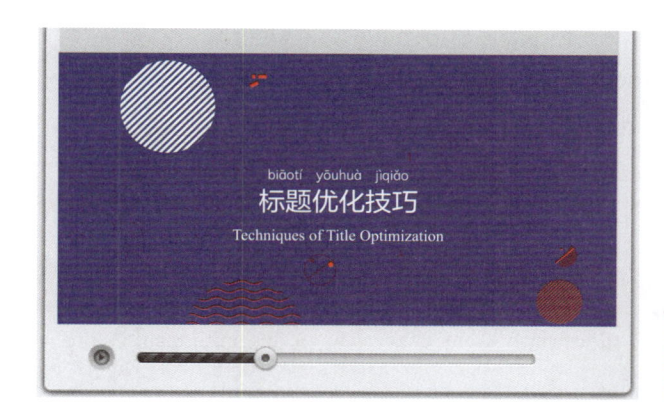

A. pǐnpái + chǎnpǐnmíng
品牌 + 产品名
brand + product name

B. màidiǎncí
卖点词
selling point terms

C. rèsōucí
热搜词
hot search terms

D. xínghào huò cānshù
型号或参数
model or parameters

Xiaomi/小米　Note 10 5G 8+128G　新品智能手机学生手机全面屏送碎屏险

五、小知识　xiǎo zhīshi　Tips

Rèsōucí
热搜词

Zài yōuhuà biāotí de shíhou, Xiāpí píngtái shang de màijiā kěyǐ tōngguò yǐxià jǐ gè
在优化标题的时候，虾皮平台上的卖家可以通过以下几个
fāngfǎ qù zhǎo yǔ chǎnpǐn xiāngguān de rèsōucí.
方法去找与产品相关的热搜词。

❶ 参考 同类目热销 商品 的标题。
Cānkǎo tóng lèimù rèxiāo shāngpǐn de biāotí.

❷ 看 市场 周报，了解最新的热搜词。
Kàn shìchǎng zhōubào, liǎojiě zuì xīn de rèsōucí.

❸ 分析虾皮大学 每月关键词推荐表。
Fēnxī Xiāpí Dàxué měi yuè guānjiàncí tuījiànbiǎo.

Hot Search Terms

When optimizing titles, sellers on Shopee platform can find hot search terms related to their products by the following means.

1. Refer to the titles of hot-selling products of the same category.
2. Read the market weekly report to know the latest hot search terms.
3. Analyze the recommended list of monthly keywords by Shopee College.

补充专业词语 bǔchōng zhuānyè cíyǔ **Supplementary Specialized Vocabulary** 🎧 04-07

1. 官方旗舰店	guānfāng qíjiàndiàn	phr.	official flagship store
2. 型号	xínghào	n.	model
3. 参数	cānshù	n.	parameter

第二部分　Part 2
汉字　Chinese Characters

一、汉字知识　Hànzì zhīshi　Knowledge about Chinese Characters

1. 汉字的笔画（4）　**Strokes of Chinese characters (4)**

笔画 Strokes	名称 Names	例字 Examples
	提 tí	习
	竖提 shùtí	衣
	横折提 héngzhétí	语
	撇点 piědiǎn	女

2. 汉字的笔顺（4）　**Stroke orders of Chinese characters (4)**

规则 Rule	例字 Examples	笔顺 Stroke orders
先外后里再封口 Outside strokes before inside strokes, and then sealing strokes	国 日	丨 冂 冂 冃 用 国 国 国 丨 冂 月 日

46

4 标题优化
Title Optimization

二、汉字认读与书写　Hànzì rèndú yǔ shūxiě　The Recognition and Writing of Chinese Characters

认读下列词语，并试着读写构成词语的汉字。
Recognize the following words, and try to read and write the Chinese characters forming these words.

热搜词　　简洁明了　　精挑细选

热		搜		词		简	
洁		明		了		精	
挑		细		选			

第三部分　Part 3
日常用语　Daily Expressions

❶ 我们机场见。Wǒmen jīchǎng jiàn. See you at the airport.
❷ 我们电话（邮件）联系。Wǒmen diànhuà (yóujiàn) liánxì. Keep in touch by phone (e-mail).
❸ 下星期一到北京的航班还有票吗？ Xià xīngqīyī dào Běijīng de hángbān hái yǒu piào ma?
　 Are there any tickets available for next Monday's flight to Beijing?

第四部分　Part 4
单元实训　Unit Practical Training

产品标题优化　chǎnpǐn biāotí yōuhuà　Product Title Optimization

实训目的 Training purpose
了解产品标题优化的目的，学习标题优化的方法，能够对产品标题进行优化。
To learn about the purpose of product title optimization, learn the methods of optimizing product titles and be able to optimize product titles.

实训组织 Training organization
每组三人，设定一个组长。
Three students in each group, with a group leader.

实训内容 Training content
❶ 各小组选定一种类目的产品，确定产品的品牌和名称。
　 Each group chooses a product of a category and decides the brand and name of the product.

❷ 小组成员到虾皮平台上搜索该产品在各个店铺的标题，每个成员分别找出两个好的产品标题和两个需要优化的标题。

The group members log on to Shopee platform to search for the titles of this product in various stores, and each member finds two good product titles and two titles that need to be optimized.

❸ 小组讨论、分析好的产品标题是如何优化的，在此基础上对需要优化的标题进行修改。

The group discusses and analyzes how the good titles are optimized and modifies the titles that need to be optimized on this basis.

❹ 各小组向全班展示优化前和优化后的产品标题，总结标题优化的意义和方法。

Each group makes a presentation of the product titles before and after optimization to the whole class, and sums up the meaning and methods of title optimization.

❺ 教师点评。

The teacher comments.

第五部分　Part 5　单元小结 Unit Summary

词语 Vocabulary

普通词语　General Vocabulary

1.	能够	nénggòu	aux.	can
2.	让	ràng	v.	let
3.	快速	kuàisù	adj.	quick
4.	了解	liǎojiě	v.	learn about, understand
5.	通常	tōngcháng	adv.	usually
6.	名	míng	n.	name
7.	决定	juédìng	v.	decide
8.	能否	néngfǒu	v.	can or cannot
9.	看到	kàndào	phr.	see
10.	是否	shìfǒu	adv.	whether... or not
11.	提升	tíshēng	v.	promote
12.	时	shí	n.	a period of time
13.	注意	zhùyì	v.	pay attention to
14.	以下	yǐxià	n.	the following
15.	三	sān	num.	three
16.	点	diǎn	m.	*used in counting items*

标题优化 4
Title Optimization

词语 cíyǔ / Vocabulary

17.	第	dì	pref.	*a prefix indicating ordinal numbers*
18.	简洁	jiǎnjié	adj.	concise
19.	明了	míngliǎo	adj.	clear
20.	可读性	kědúxìng	n.	readability
21.	强	qiáng	adj.	strong, resolute
22.	突出	tūchū	v.	lay emphasis on
23.	精挑细选	jīngtiāo-xìxuǎn	phr.	carefully select

专业词语 Specialized Vocabulary

1.	标题	biāotí	n.	title
2.	热搜词	rèsōucí	n.	hot search term
3.	卖点词	màidiǎncí	n.	selling point term
	卖点	màidiǎn	n.	selling point
4.	浏览者	liúlǎnzhě	n.	viewer
5.	优化	yōuhuà	v.	optimize
6.	搜索	sōusuǒ	v.	search
7.	流量	liúliàng	n.	traffic, volume of flow
8.	点击率	diǎnjīlǜ	n.	click-through rate

补充专业词语 Supplementary Specialized Vocabulary

1.	官方旗舰店	guānfāng qíjiàndiàn	phr.	official flagship store
2.	型号	xínghào	n.	model
3.	参数	cānshù	n.	parameter

句子 jùzi / Sentences

1. 好的产品标题通常包括品牌名、产品名、热搜词和卖点词。
2. 标题优化可以提升产品的搜索流量和点击率。
3. 标题要简洁明了，可读性强。
4. 标题要突出产品的卖点和优势。
5. 关键词要精挑细选。
6. 关键词要与产品高度相关，不要用无效关键词。

5

Zhǔtú yōuhuà
主图优化
Main Image Optimization

zhǔtú yōuhuà
主图 优化
Main Image Optimization

zhǔtú qīngxī
主图清晰
The Main Images Should Be Clear

wén'àn jiǎnjié
文案 简洁
The Copy Should Be Concise

túwén-bìngmào
图文并茂
The Images Should Be Beautifully Illustrated

51

中文＋电子商务（中级）

> **题解　Introduction**
>
> 1. 学习内容：主图优化的目的和注意点。
>   Learning content: The purpose and important points of main image optimization.
> 2. 知识目标：学习与主图优化相关的关键词，学习汉字的笔画"㇏""㇋""㇀""乁"和独体结构，学写本单元相关汉字。
>   Knowledge objectives: To master the keywords related to main image optimization, learn the strokes "㇏", "㇋", "㇀", "乁" and independent structure of Chinese characters, and write the characters related to this unit.
> 3. 技能目标：学会优化主图
>   Skill objectives: To learn to optimize main images.

第一部分　Part 1

课文　Texts

一、热身　rèshēn　Warm-up

1. 给词语选择对应的图片。Choose the corresponding pictures for the words.

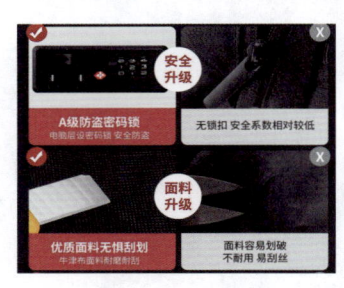

A.

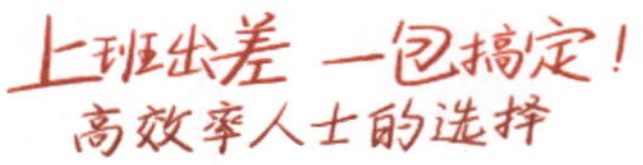

B.

C.

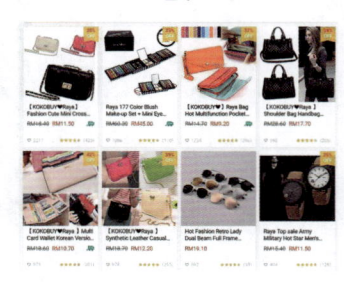

D.

52

主图优化
Main Image Optimization 5

① fēngmiàntú
封面图 ＿＿＿＿＿＿＿＿
cover image

② xìjiétú
细节图 ＿＿＿＿＿＿＿＿
detail image

③ xiángqíngyè
详情页 ＿＿＿＿＿＿＿＿
detail page

④ wén'àn
文案 ＿＿＿＿＿＿＿＿
copy

2. 看视频，判断下列关于虾皮平台上产品主图的说法是否正确。
Watch the video and decide whether the following statements about product main images on Shopee platform are true or false.

① Chǎnpǐn zhǔtú zuì duō shàngchuán jiǔ zhāng.
产品 主图 最多 上 传 九 张。（　　）
Nine product main images can be uploaded at most.

② Dì-yī zhāng zhǔtú jiào fēngmiàntú.
第一 张 主图 叫 封面图。（　　）
The first main image is called cover image.

③ Zhǔtú bù néng shàngchuán shìpín.
主图 不能 上 传 视频。（　　）
Videos can't be uploaded as main images.

④ Zhǔtú yōuhuà shì wèile xīyǐn gùkè, tíshēng diǎnjīlǜ.
主图 优化 是 为了 吸引 顾客，提升 点击率。（　　）
The main image optimization is to attract customers and increase click-through rate.

53

二、课文 kèwén Texts

A 05-01

Mǎijiā shūrù guānjiàncí jìnxíng sōusuǒ shí, huì chūxiàn hěn duō xiāngguān chǎnpǐn de fēngmiàntú. Fēngmiàntú shì mǎijiā duì chǎnpǐn de dì-yī yìnxiàng. Yì zhāng hǎo de fēngmiàntú, néng ràng mǎijiā yǒu diǎnjī, chákàn chǎnpǐn xiángqíngyè de yùwàng.

买家输入关键词进行搜索时，会出现很多相关产品的封面图。封面图是买家对产品的第一印象。一张好的封面图，能让买家有点击、查看产品详情页的欲望。

译文 yìwén Text in English

When the buyers enter the keywords to search, many cover images of related products will appear. The cover image is the first impression of a product on the buyers. A good cover image can arouse the buyers' desire to click and view the detail page of the product.

普通词语 pǔtōng cíyǔ General Vocabulary 05-02

1.	输入	shūrù	v.	input
2.	出现	chūxiàn	v.	appear
3.	相关	xiāngguān	v.	be related to
4.	对	duì	prep.	to
5.	印象	yìnxiàng	n.	impression
6.	查看	chákàn	v.	check, inspect
7.	欲望	yùwàng	n.	desire

专业词语 zhuānyè cíyǔ Specialized Vocabulary 05-03

1.	封面图	fēngmiàntú	n.	cover image
2.	详情页	xiángqíngyè	n.	detail page

B 05-04

Zhǔtú li de chǎnpǐn túpiàn yào qīngxī, wén'àn yào jiǎnjié. Zhǔtú yīnggāi zhǎnshì
主图里的产品图片要清晰，文案要简洁。主图应该展示

chǎnpǐn de gōngnéng、kuǎnshì、shǐyòng xiàoguǒ、xìjié děng fāngmiàn de nèiróng. Tōngguò
产品的功能、款式、使用效果、细节等方面的内容。通过

zhǔtú cèshì, wǒmen bǎ diǎnjīlǜ zuì gāo de túpiàn zuòchéng fēngmiàntú.
主图测试，我们把点击率最高的图片做成封面图。

译文 yìwén Text in English

The product images in main images should be clear and the copy should be concise. The main images should showcase the function, style, use effect, and details of the product. Through main image test, we make the one with the highest click-through rates the cover image.

普通词语 pǔtōng cíyǔ General Vocabulary 05-05

1.	清晰	qīngxī	adj.	clear
2.	展示	zhǎnshì	v.	show, present
3.	使用	shǐyòng	v.	use
4.	方面	fāngmiàn	n.	aspect
5.	内容	nèiróng	n.	content
6.	把	bǎ	prep.	*used to put the object before the verb*
7.	最	zuì	adv.	most
8.	高	gāo	adj.	high
9.	做	zuò	v.	make
10.	成	chéng	v.	become

专业词语 zhuānyè cíyǔ Specialized Vocabulary				05-06
1.	主图	zhǔtú	n.	main image
2.	文案	wén'àn	n.	copy
3.	功能	gōngnéng	n.	function
4.	款式	kuǎnshì	n.	style
5.	效果	xiàoguǒ	n.	effect
6.	细节	xìjié	n.	detail
7.	测试	cèshì	v.	test

三、视听说 shì-tīng-shuō Viewing, Listening and Speaking

1. 看视频，了解产品主图优化的要点，判断下列哪张图片最适合做封面图，并试着说出你的理由。
Watch the video to learn about the key points of product main image optimization, decide which of the following pictures is the most suitable for being the cover image, and try to explain your reasons.

❶ Zhǔtú yào qīngxī, yídìng yào tūchū chǎnpǐn.
主图要清晰，一定要突出产品。
The main images must be clear and highlight the product.

❷ Wén'àn yào jiǎnjié, bù néng xìnxī guòzài.
文案要简洁，不能信息过载。
The copy should be concise, without information overload.

❸ Màidiǎn tūchū, túwén-bìngmào.
卖点突出，图文并茂。
The selling points should be highlighted and the images should be beautifully illustrated.

A.　　B.　　C.　　D.

Zuì shìhé zuò fēngmiàntú de shì:
最适合做封面图的是：(　　)
The one that is the most suitable for being the cover image is:

2. 说一说 Let's talk

模仿说出主图优化的要点。 Name the key points of main image optimization following the video.

四、学以致用 xuéyǐzhìyòng Practicing What You Have Learnt

看视频，学习主图需要展示的产品内容，将下列内容与所给图片匹配连线。
Watch the video to learn the product content that needs to be shown in the main images, and match and match the following content with the given pictures.

选择主图
xuǎnzé zhǔtú
Select Main Images

① kuǎnshì 款式 style
② xìjié 细节 detail
③ gōngnéng 功能 function
④ shǐyòng xiàoguǒ 使用效果 use effect

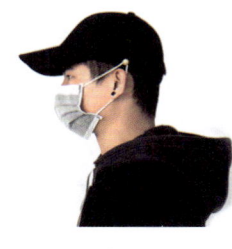

A.    B.    C. 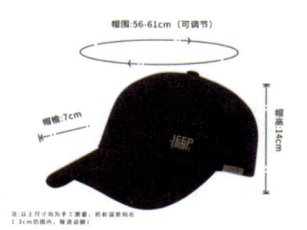   D.

五、小知识 xiǎo zhīshi Tips

移动端 主图
Yídòngduān zhǔtú

移动端使用的流量远多于电脑端，因此做产品主图时要充分考虑移动端的特点。你的图片越大，买家浏览时花费的流量越多，加载速度越慢，特别是在非 Wi-Fi 上网的情况下。所以，

zhǔtú　bú shì túpiàn pǐnzhì yuè gāo yuè hǎo,　ér shì　yǐ néng zài shǒujīduān qīngxī zhǎnshì,　dǎkāi
主图不是图片品质越高越好，而是以能在手机端清晰展示、打开

bù　kǎ wéi zuì jiā xiàoguǒ.
不卡为最佳效果。

Main Images on Mobile Terminals

Mobile terminals use far more data than computer terminals, so the characteristics of mobile terminals should be taken into full account when making product main images. The larger your images are, the more data the buyers use during viewing, and the lower the loading speed is, especially when no WiFi connection is available. Therefore, for the main images, it's not the higher the image quality is, the better, instead, the best effect is that they can be clearly shown on mobile terminals and opened without lag.

补充专业词语 bǔchōng zhuānyè cíyǔ Supplementary Specialized Vocabulary　05-07

1.	细节图	xìjiétú	n.	detail image
2.	信息过载	xìnxī guòzài	phr.	information overload
3.	图文并茂	túwén-bìngmào	phr.	be excellent in both illustrations and texts

第二部分　Part 2　汉字　Chinese Characters

一、汉字知识　Hànzì zhīshi　Knowledge about Chinese Characters

1. 汉字的笔画（5）Strokes of Chinese characters (5)

笔画 Strokes	名称 Names	例字 Examples
㇂	斜钩 xiégōu	我
㇌	卧钩 wògōu	心
㇆	横折钩 héngzhégōu	问
㇈	横折弯钩 héngzhéwāngōu	几

2. 汉字的结构（1）Structures of Chinese characters (1)

结构类型 Structure type	例字 Examples	结构图示 Illustration
独体结构 Independent structure	生 不	□

二、汉字认读与书写　Hànzì rèndú yǔ shūxiě　The Recognition and Writing of Chinese Characters

认读下列词语，并试着读写构成词语的汉字。
Recognize the following words, and try to read and write the Chinese characters forming these words.

文案简洁　　产品功能　　使用效果

文			案			简			洁	
产			品			功			能	
使			用			效			果	

第三部分　Part 3　日常用语 Daily Expressions

❶ 我要两张 11 号到上海的火车票。Wǒ yào liǎng zhāng 11 hào dào Shànghǎi de huǒchēpiào.
I want two train tickets to Shanghai on the 11th.

❷ 我的护照和钱包都丢了。Wǒ de hùzhào hé qiánbāo dōu diū le. I've lost both my passport and wallet.

❸ 还可以便宜一些吗？Hái kěyǐ piányi yìxiē ma? Can you make it cheaper?

第四部分　Part 4　单元实训 Unit Practical Training

产品主图优化与点击率调研　chǎnpǐn zhǔtú yōuhuà yǔ diǎnjīlǜ diàoyán
Research on Product Main Image Optimization and Click-through Rate

实训目的 Training purpose

了解产品主图优化的要点，学会优化主图，提升产品点击率。
To understand the key points of product main image optimization, learn to optimize main images and improve click-through rates of products.

实训组织 Training organization

每组三人，设定一个组长。
Three students in each group, with a group leader.

实训内容 Training content

❶ 学习产品主图优化的要点和方法。
Learn the key points and methods of product main image optimization.

（1）主图要清晰，突出产品。

The main images should be clear and highlight the product.

（2）文案要简洁，文字信息不能过多。

The copy should be concise without too much text information.

（3）主图要展示出产品的外观、功能、款式、细节、使用效果等信息，让买家快速了解产品。

The main images should showcase the appearance, function, style, details, use effect, etc. of the product to let the buyers know about the product quickly.

（4）主图要突出产品的卖点，有吸引力。

The main images should be attractive and highlight the selling points of the product.

❷ 每组选定一种产品，组员们到虾皮平台上输入关键词进行搜索，查看产品的封面图和其他主图，分析点击率高、销量好的产品是如何进行主图优化的。

Each group chooses a kind of product. The group members log on to Shopee platform and enter keywords to search for it, check the cover images and other main images of the products, and analyze how the products with high click-through rates and sales conduct main image optimization.

❸ 各小组选取本组产品最具代表性的主图，在班级进行陈述，总结主图优化的要点和方法。

Each group selects the most typical main images of the group's product to make a presentation to the whole class, and sums up the key points and methods of main image optimization.

❹ 教师点评。

The teacher comments.

第五部分　Part 5

单元小结　Unit Summary

普通词语　General Vocabulary

cíyǔ
词语
Vocabulary

1.	输入	shūrù	v.	input
2.	出现	chūxiàn	v.	appear
3.	相关	xiāngguān	v.	be related to
4.	对	duì	prep.	to
5.	印象	yìnxiàng	n.	impression
6.	查看	chákàn	v.	check, inspect
7.	欲望	yùwàng	n.	desire
8.	清晰	qīngxī	adj.	clear
9.	展示	zhǎnshì	v.	show, present
10.	使用	shǐyòng	v.	use
11.	方面	fāngmiàn	n.	aspect

词语 Vocabulary

12.	内容	nèiróng	n.	content
13.	把	bǎ	prep.	*used to put the object before the verb*
14.	最	zuì	adv.	most
15.	高	gāo	adj.	high
16.	做	zuò	v.	make
17.	成	chéng	v.	become

专业词语 Specialized Vocabulary

1.	封面图	fēngmiàntú	n.	cover image
2.	详情页	xiángqíngyè	n.	detail page
3.	主图	zhǔtú	n.	main image
4.	文案	wén'àn	n.	copy
5.	功能	gōngnéng	n.	function
6.	款式	kuǎnshì	n.	style
7.	效果	xiàoguǒ	n.	effect
8.	细节	xìjié	n.	detail
9.	测试	cèshì	v.	test

补充专业词语 Supplementary Specialized Vocabulary

1.	细节图	xìjiétú	n.	detail image
2.	信息过载	xìnxī guòzài	phr.	information overload
3.	图文并茂	túwén-bìngmào	phr.	be excellent in both illustrations and texts

句子 Sentences

1. 虾皮上最多上传九张产品主图，第一张叫封面图。
2. 主图不仅可以上传图片，也可以上传视频。
3. 主图优化是为了吸引买家，提升点击率。
4. 封面图是买家对产品的第一印象，一张好的封面图能吸引买家点击、查看产品详情页。
6. 主图的产品图片要清晰，文案要简洁。
7. 主图应该展示产品的功能、款式、细节、使用效果等方面的内容。

6

Zhàn nèi yǐnliú
站内引流
On-site Traffic Driving

guānjiàncí guǎnggào
关键词 广告
Keyword Advertisements

zhàn nèi yǐnliú de guǎnggào fāngshì
站内引流的 广告 方式
Advertising Methods of On-site Traffic Driving

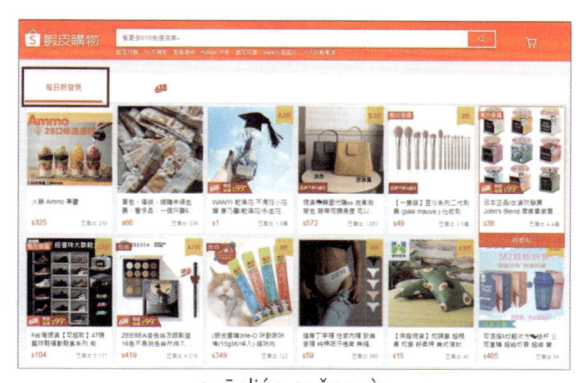

guānlián guǎnggào
关联 广告
Discovery advertisements

diànpù guǎnggào
店铺 广告
Store Advertisements

63

题解 Introduction

1. 学习内容：了解站内引流的方式。
   Learning content: To learn about the methods of on-site traffic driving.
2. 知识目标：掌握与站内引流相关的关键词，学习汉字的笔画"㇇""㇌"和品字形结构，学写本单元相关汉字。
   Knowledge objectives: To master the keywords related to on-site traffic driving, learn the strokes "㇇", "㇌", and 品-shaped structure of Chinese characters, and write the characters related to this unit.
3. 技能目标：学会进行站内引流。
   Skill objectives: To learn to conduct on-site traffic driving.

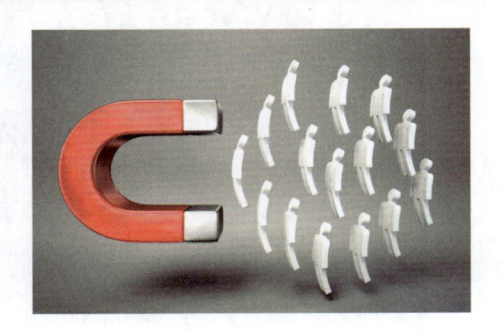

第一部分 Part 1

课文 Texts

一、热身 rèshēn Warm-up

1. 给词语选择对应的图片。 Choose the corresponding pictures for the words.

A.

B.

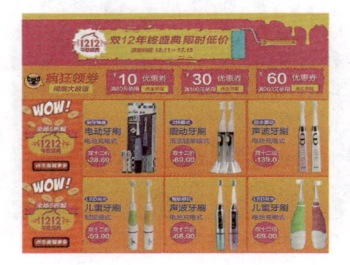

C.

D.

站内引流
On-site Traffic Driving 6

① biāotí yōuhuà
标题 优化 _____
title optimization

② guānjiàncí yōuhuà
关键词 优化 _____
keyword optimization

③ guānlián yíngxiāo
关联 营销 _____
related marketing

④ cùxiāo huódòng
促销 活动 _____
sales promotion activity

2. 看视频，了解站内引流的方式，为相关视频选择正确的选项。
Watch the videos to learn about the methods of on-site traffic driving, and choose the right options for the related videos.

zhàn nèi yǐnliú de fāngshì
站内引流的方式
Methods of On-site Traffic Driving

A. shèzhì qítā xiāngguān shāngpǐn tuījiàn de liànjiē
设置其他 相 关 商品 推荐的 链接
set up links recommending other related products

B. dàxíng cùxiāo huódòng
大型 促销 活 动
large sales promotion activities

C. shèzhì diànpù rèmài shāngpǐn de liànjiē
设置 店铺 热卖 商品 的 链接
set up links of hot-selling products in the store

D. fù yóu shìyòng
付邮 试用
pay postage for product trials

① ▶ (　) ② ▶ (　) ③ ▶ (　) ④ ▶ (　)

65

二、课文　kèwén　Texts

A　06-01

Màijiā kěyǐ lìyòng zhàn nèi yǐnliú de fāngshì tíshēng diànpù de rénqì. Zhàn nèi yǐnliú
卖家可以利用站内引流的方式提升店铺的人气。站内引流
yìbān fēnwéi miǎnfèi yǐnliú hé fùfèi yǐnliú. Qízhōng, biāotí yōuhuà shǔyú miǎnfèi yǐnliú,
一般分为免费引流和付费引流。其中，标题优化属于免费引流，
guǎnggào shǔyú fùfèi yǐnliú.
广告属于付费引流。

译文　yìwén　Text in English

Sellers can enhance the popularity of the store through the method of on-site traffic driving. The method of on-site traffic driving is generally divided into free traffic driving and paid traffic driving. Among them, title optimization falls under free traffic driving, and advertising falls under paid traffic driving.

普通词语　pǔtōng cíyǔ　General Vocabulary　06-02

1.	利用	lìyòng	v.	utilize
2.	站内	zhàn nèi	phr.	on-site
3.	人气	rénqì	n.	popularity
4.	一般	yìbān	adj.	general, ordinary
5.	属于	shǔyú	v.	belong to

专业词语　zhuānyè cíyǔ　Specialized Vocabulary　06-03

1.	免费引流	miǎnfèi yǐnliú	phr.	free traffic driving
2.	付费引流	fùfèi yǐnliú	phr.	paid traffic driving
	付费	fùfèi	v.	pay

B 🎧 06-04

Guǎnggào shì Xiāpí zhàn nèi yǐnliú de zhòngyào fāngshì. Xiāpí guǎnggào fēnwéi
广告是虾皮站内引流的重要方式。虾皮广告分为

guānjiàncí guǎnggào、guānlián guǎnggào hé diànpù guǎnggào. Guǎnggào zhǐyǒu zài yònghù diǎnjī shí,
关键词广告、关联广告和店铺广告。广告只有在用户点击时,

shāngjiā cái huì bèi shōufèi, dānchún xiǎnshì shì miǎnfèi de.
商家才会被收费,单纯显示是免费的。

译文 yìwén Text in English

Advertising is an important way of on-site traffic driving on Shopee. Advertisements on Shopee are divided into keyword advertisements, discovery advertisements and store advertisements. Sellers are only charged when users click on the advertisements, and mere display is free of charge.

普通词语 pǔtōng cíyǔ General Vocabulary 🎧 06-05

1.	点击	diǎnjī	v.	click
2.	单纯	dānchún	adj.	pure, mere

专业词语 zhuānyè cíyǔ Specialized Vocabulary 🎧 06-06

1.	用户	yònghù	n.	user
2.	收费	shōufèi	v.	charge
3.	显示	xiǎnshì	v.	display

中文 + 电子商务（中级）

三、视听说　shì-tīng-shuō　Viewing, Listening and Speaking

1. 看视频，了解电商站内引流的广告方式，将视频叙述与相关选项相连，并模仿说出电商的站内引流如何通过广告进行。

Watch the videos to understand advertising methods of on-site traffic driving on e-commerce platforms, match the videos narratives with related options, and talk about how on-site traffic driving on e-commerce platforms can be carried out through advertising following the videos.

diànshāng zhàn nèi yǐnliú de guǎnggào fāngshì
电商 站内引流的广告方式
Advertising Methods of On-site Traffic Driving on E-commerce Platforms

A. guānjiàncí guǎnggào
关键词 广告
keyword advertisements

B. diànpù guǎnggào
店铺 广告
store advertisements

C. guānlián guǎnggào
关联 广告
discovery advertisements

① ▶　　②	▶　　③ ▶

2. 说一说　Let's talk

模仿说出电商平台站内引流的方式。　**Name the ways of on-site traffic driving on e-commerce platforms following the videos.**

四、学以致用　xuéyǐzhìyòng　Practicing What You Have Learnt

看视频，学习虾皮平台站内引流广告的使用方式，为下列广告投放操作步骤排序。
Watch the video to learn the ways of using advertisements for on-site traffic driving on Shopee platform, and arrange the steps of the following advertisement serving operations in order.

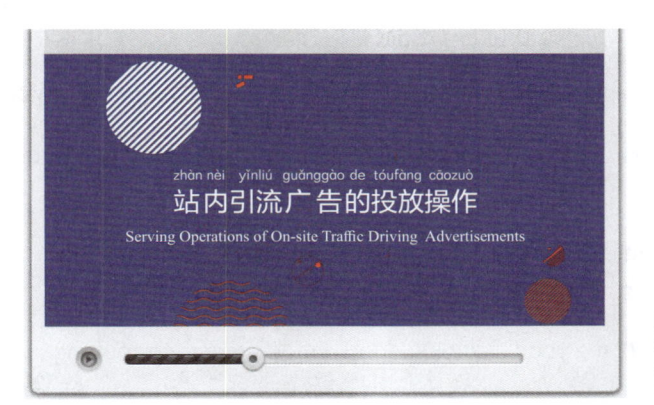

A. Guǎnggào yùrè, zhùlì diànpù yíngjiē gòuwù gāofēngqī.
广告预热，助力店铺迎接购物高峰期。
Warm up through advertisements to help the store meet the shopping peak.

B. Jiānkòng guǎnggào chéngxiào.
监控广告成效。
Monitor the advertising effectiveness.

C. Yùnyòng guǎnggào tíshēng xiāoliàng.
运用广告提升销量。
Use advertisements to boost sales.

D. Gěi guǎnggào zhànghù chōngzhí.
给广告账户充值。
Top up your advertising account.

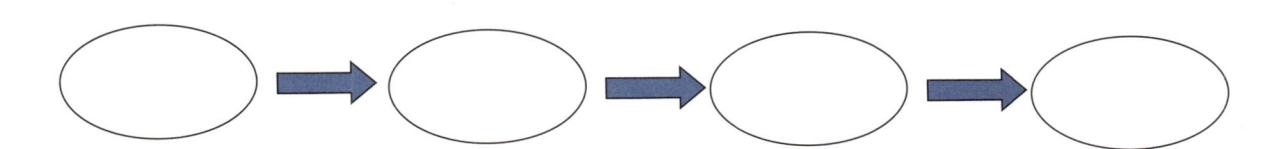

○ → ○ → ○ → ○

五、小知识　xiǎo zhīshi　Tips

虾皮广告的预算设定
Xiāpí guǎnggào de yùsuàn shèdìng

设定广告预算可以确保广告花费不超过设定的钱数。
Shèdìng guǎnggào yùsuàn kěyǐ quèbǎo guǎnggào huāfèi bù chāoguò shèdìng de qiánshù.

a. 例如：每日预算为3美元，代表每天的广告花费超过3美元之后，广告会停止投放。
Lìrú: Měi rì yùsuàn wéi 3 měiyuán, dàibiǎo měi tiān de guǎnggào huāfèi chāoguò 3 měiyuán zhīhòu, guǎnggào huì tíngzhǐ tóufàng.

b. 例如：总预算为10美元，代表当您的广告投放期间的总花费超过10美元之后，广告会停止投放。
Lìrú: Zǒng yùsuàn wéi 10 měiyuán, dàibiǎo dāng nín de guǎnggào tóufàng qījiān de zǒng huāfèi chāoguò 10 měiyuán zhīhòu, guǎnggào huì tíngzhǐ tóufàng.

Budget Setting of Advertisements on Shopee

Setting an advertising budget can ensure that advertising expenditure does not exceed the set amount of money.

a. For example: a daily budget of $3 means that advertisement serving will stop after the daily advertising expenditure exceeds $3.

b. For example: a total budget of $10 means that advertisement serving will stop after your total expenditure exceeds $10 during the advertisement serving period.

补充专业词语　bǔchōng zhuānyè cíyǔ　Supplementary Specialized Vocabulary　06-07

1.	关联营销	guānlián yíngxiāo	phr.	related marketing
2.	付邮试用	fù yóu shìyòng	phr.	pay postage for product trial
3.	预算设定	yùsuàn shèdìng	phr.	budget setting
4.	广告投放	guǎnggào tóufàng	phr.	advertisement serving
5.	广告花费	guǎnggào huāfèi	phr.	advertising expenditure

第二部分　Part 2　汉字　Chinese Characters

一、汉字知识　Hànzì zhīshi　Knowledge about Chinese Characters

1. 汉字的笔画（6）　Strokes of Chinese characters (6)

笔画 Strokes	名称 Names	例字 Examples
㇌	横撇弯钩 héngpiěwāngōu	部
㇅	横折折折钩 héngzhézhézhégōu	奶

2. 汉字的结构（2）　Structures of Chinese characters (2)

结构类型 Structure type	例字 Example	结构图示 Illustration
品字形结构 品-shaped structure	品	⊟

二、汉字认读与书写　Hànzì rèndú yǔ shūxiě　The Recognition and Writing of Chinese Characters

认读下列词语，并试着读写构成词语的汉字。
Recognize the following words, and try to read and write the Chinese characters forming these words.

站内引流　　店铺广告　　标题优化

站		内		引		流	
店		铺		广		告	
标		题		优		化	

第三部分　Part 3　日常用语　Daily Expressions

❶ 请原谅。Qǐng yuánliàng. Pardon me, please./ Forgive me, please.
❷ 不好意思，麻烦你……Bù hǎoyìsi, máfan nǐ… Excuse me, could you please...
❸ 我前几天感冒了。Wǒ qián jǐ tiān gǎnmào le. I had a cold several days ago.

第四部分　Part 4　单元实训 Unit Practical Training

电商平台站内引流广告的使用　diànshāng píngtái zhàn nèi yǐnliú guǎnggào de shǐyòng
Use of On-site Traffic Driving Advertisements on E-commerce Platforms

实训目的 Training purpose

了解电商平台站内引流广告的使用方式以及广告预算的设置，能够了解并使用广告进行引流。

To understand the ways of using on-site traffic driving advertisements on e-commerce platforms and the setting of advertising budget, and be able to understand and use advertising for driving traffic.

实训组织 Training organization

每组三人，设定一个组长。

Three students in each group, with a group leader.

实训内容 Training content

❶ 虾皮平台站内引流广告的使用。

Use of on-site traffic driving advertisements on Shopee platform.

（1）在购物高峰前投放广告。

　　Advertise before the shopping peak.

（2）给广告账户充值。

　　Top up the advertising account.

（3）设置广告预算。

　　Set advertising budget.

（4）投放广告，提升销量。

　　Advertise to increase sales volume.

❷ 虾皮平台站内引流广告的优化。

　　Optimization of on-site traffic driving advertisements on Shopee platform.

（1）监控广告成效。

　　Monitor the effectiveness of advertising.

（2）优化商品详情页。

　　Optimize the product's detail page.

（3）优化店铺效果。

　　Optimize the store effect.

❸ 各组汇报广告设计及优化效果。

　　Each group reports the advertisement design and optimization effect.

❹ 教师点评。

　　The teacher comments.

第五部分 Part 5

单元小结 Unit Summary

词语 / Vocabulary

普通词语　General Vocabulary

1.	利用	lìyòng	v.	utilize
2.	站内	zhàn nèi	phr.	on-site
3.	人气	rénqì	n.	popularity
4.	一般	yìbān	adj.	general, ordinary
5.	属于	shǔyú	v.	belong to
6.	点击	diǎnjī	v.	click
7.	单纯	dānchún	adj.	pure, mere

专业词语　Specialized Vocabulary

1.	免费引流	miǎnfèi yǐnliú	phr.	free traffic driving
2.	付费引流	fùfèi yǐnliú	phr.	paid traffic driving
	付费	fùfèi	v.	pay
3.	用户	yònghù	n.	user
4.	收费	shōufèi	v.	charge
5.	显示	xiǎnshì	v.	display

补充专业词语　Supplementary Specialized Vocabulary

1.	关联营销	guānlián yíngxiāo	phr.	related marketing
2.	付邮试用	fù yóu shìyòng	phr.	pay postage for product trial
3.	预算设定	yùsuàn shèdìng	phr.	budget setting
4.	广告投放	guǎnggào tóufàng	phr.	advertisement serving
5.	广告花费	guǎnggào huāfèi	phr.	advertising expenditure

句子 / Sentences

1. 卖家可以利用站内引流的方式提升店铺的人气。
2. 站内引流一般分为免费引流和付费引流。
3. 标题优化属于免费引流。
4. 广告属于付费引流。
5. 虾皮广告分为关键词广告、关联广告和店铺广告。
6. 广告只有在用户点击时，商家才会被收费。
7. 广告显示是免费的。

7

Diànpù cùxiāo
店铺促销
Sales Promotion of Stores

diànpù cùxiāo de fāngshì
店铺促销的方式
Ways of Sales Promotion of Stores

yùnfèi zhékòu
运费 折扣
Freight Discount

shāngpǐn bāoyóu
商品 包邮
Free Shipping of Goods

tàozhuāng yōuhuì
套装 优惠
Bundle Deals

mǎi yī sòng yī
买一送一
Buy One and Get One Free

75

题解　Introduction

1. 学习内容：电商平台的店铺促销。
   Learning content: Store promotion on e-commerce platforms.
2. 知识目标：掌握与店铺促销相关的关键词，学习汉字的笔画"勹""乀"和上下结构、上中下结构，学写本单元相关汉字。
   Knowledge objectives: To master the keywords related to store promotion, to learn the strokes "勹", "乀", top-bottom structure and top-middle-bottom structure of Chinese characters, and write the characters related to this unit.
3. 技能目标：掌握店铺促销的方式和手段。
   Skill objectives: To master the methods and means of store promotion.

第一部分　Part 1

课文　Texts

一、热身　rèshēn　Warm-up

1. 给词语选择对应的图片。 Choose the corresponding pictures for the words.

A.　　　　B.　　　　C.　　　　D.

❶ 折扣 zhékòu _____
discount

❷ 优惠券 yōuhuìquàn _____
coupon

❸ 限时折扣 xiànshí zhékòu _____
discount in limited time

❹ 关注礼 guānzhùlǐ _____
rewards for following

店铺促销 7
Sales Promotion of Stores

2. 看视频，了解店铺促销的方式，为相关视频选择正确选项。
Watch the videos to learn about ways of sales promotion of stores, and choose the right options for the related videos.

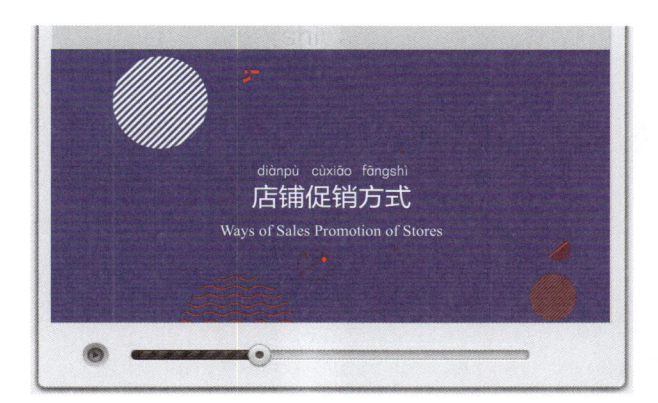

diànpù cùxiāo fāngshì
店铺促销方式
Ways of Sales Promotion of Stores

    yùnfèi zhékòu
A. 运费折扣
   freight discount

    shāngpǐn bāo yóu
B. 商品包邮
   free shipping of goods

    mǎi yī sòng yī
C. 买一送一
   buy one and get one free

    tàozhuāng yōuhuì
D. 套装优惠
   bundle deals

① ▶ (　　)   ② ▶ (　　)   ③ ▶ (　　)   ④ ▶ (　　)

二、课文　kèwén　Texts

A 🎧 07-01

Zhékòu huódòng shì zài shāngpǐn yuánjià jīchǔ shang dǎzhé, ràng gùkè juéde gèng shíhuì.
折扣活动是在商品原价基础上打折，让顾客觉得更实惠。

Shāngpǐn shǒuyè huì xǐngmù de zhǎnshì zhékòu xìnxī, yǒulì yú xīyǐn gùkè shìxiàn.
商品首页会醒目地展示折扣信息，有利于吸引顾客视线。

快乐五一，[我买嘛]将放价进行到底！
精彩连连，折扣多多，赶快行动吧！

77

中文 + 电子商务（中级）

译文 yìwén Text in English

Discount activities are to give discount on the basis of the original price of goods to make customers feel more affordable. The discount information is displayed prominently on the home page of goods, which is conducive to catching customers' attention.

普通词语 pǔtōng cíyǔ General Vocabulary 🎧 07-02

1.	基础	jīchǔ	n.	basis
2.	觉得	juéde	v.	feel
3.	实惠	shíhuì	adj.	substantial
4.	首页	shǒuyè	n.	home page
5.	醒目	xǐngmù	adj.	eye-catching
6.	有利于	yǒulì yú	phr.	be beneficial to
7.	视线	shìxiàn	n.	line of vision/sight

专业词语 zhuānyè cíyǔ Specialized Vocabulary 🎧 07-03

1.	折扣	zhékòu	n.	discount
2.	原价	yuánjià	n.	original price

B 🎧 07-04

Yōuhuìquàn bù gǎibiàn shāngpǐn yuánjià. Gùkè tōngguò zhǔdòng diǎnjī lǐng quàn de fāngshì,
优惠券不改变商品原价。顾客通过主动点击领券的方式，

zài xiàdān shí zìdòng dǐkòu、jiǎnmiǎn yídìng shùliàng de jīn'é, cóng'ér huòdé gèng shíhuì de
在下单时自动抵扣、减免一定数量的金额，从而获得更实惠的

jiàgé.
价格。

译文 yìwén Text in English

Coupons do not change the original price of the goods. By taking the initiative to click and get coupons, a certain amount of money is deducted or reduced automatically when customers place an order, so that they get more favorable prices.

7 店铺促销
Sales Promotion of Stores

普通词语 pǔtōng cíyǔ General Vocabulary 🎧 07-05

1.	改变	gǎibiàn	v.	change
2.	主动	zhǔdòng	adj.	taking the initiative
3.	自动	zìdòng	adv.	automatically
4.	一定	yídìng	adj.	certain
5.	数量	shùliàng	n.	quantity
6.	从而	cóng'ér	conj.	thus

专业词语 zhuānyè cíyǔ Specialized Vocabulary 🎧 07-06

1.	优惠券	yōuhuìquàn	n.	coupon
2.	领券	lǐng quàn	phr.	get a coupon
3.	抵扣	dǐkòu	v.	deduct
4.	减免	jiǎnmiǎn	v.	exempt and reduce

三、视听说 shì-tīng-shuō Viewing, Listening and Speaking

1. 看视频，了解运费折扣促销的两种类型，为相关视频选择正确的选项，并模仿说出运费折扣促销的不同类型。

Watch the videos to learn about the two types of freight discount promotion, choose the right options for the related videos, and name the different types of freight discount promotion following the videos.

yùnfèi zhékòu cùxiāo
运费折扣促销
Freight Discount Promotion

A. shèzhì miǎn yùn ménkǎn
设置 免 运 门槛
set a threshold for free shipping

① ▶ (　　)

B. wú ménkǎn miǎn yùn
无 门槛 免 运
no threshold for free shipping

② ▶ (　　)

79

2. 说一说   Let's talk

模仿说出电商平台的运费促销方式。   Name the ways of freight promotion of e-commerce platforms following the videos.

四、学以致用   xuéyǐzhìyòng   Practicing What You Have Learnt

看视频学习虾皮店铺优惠券的各种类型，根据图片给相关视频选择正确的分类选项。
Watch the videos to learn the different types of coupons of Shopee stores, and choose the right classification options for the related videos according to the pictures.

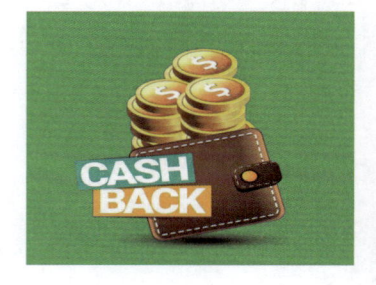

Xiāpí diànpù yōuhuìquàn
虾皮店铺优惠券
Coupons of Shopee Stores

A. xiànjīn fǎnhuán
现金返还
cashback
① ( )

B. zhékòu (bǎifēnbǐ)
折扣（百分比）
discount (percentage)
② ( )

C. zhékòu (gùdìng jīn'é)
折扣（固定金额）
discount (fixed amount)
③ ( )

五、小知识   xiǎo zhīshi   Tips

Diànshāng píngtái de zhékòu huódòng
电商平台的折扣活动

Zhékòu huódòng zhǐ zài shāngpǐn yuánjià jīchǔ shang dǎzhé. Rúguǒ shāngpǐn de jiàgé zài
折扣活动指在商品原价基础上打折。如果商品的价格在
qī tiān zhīnèi shàngtiáoguo, cǐshí màijiā chóngxīn shèzhì shāngpǐn de zhékòu jiàgé, jiù huì bèi
七天之内上调过，此时卖家重新设置商品的折扣价格，就会被

Xiāpí píngtái pàndìng wéi xūjiǎ zhékòu. Suǒyǐ, rúguǒ yùnyíng rényuán xūyào tiáozhěng jiàgé,
虾皮平台 判定 为 虚假 折扣。所以，如果 运营 人员 需要 调整 价格，
zuìhǎo shì zà qī tiān zhīhòu, huò jiāng shāngpǐn de jiàgé tiáozhěng wéi yuánjià hòu zài chóngxīn shèzhì
最好是在七天之后，或将 商品的价格 调整 为原价后再 重新 设置
zhékòu jiàgé.
折扣价格。

Discount Activities on E-commerce Platforms

Discount activities refer to making discount on the basis of the original price of goods. If the price of goods has been increased within seven days and the seller resets the discount price of goods now, it will be judged by Shopee platform as a false discount. Therefore, if the operators need to adjust the price, they preferably do it after seven days, or they can adjust the price of goods to the original price and then reset the discount price.

补充专业词语 bǔchōng zhuānyè cíyǔ Supplementary Specialized Vocabulary 🎧 07-07

1.	运费折扣	yùnfèi zhékòu	phr.	freight discount
2.	商品包邮	shāngpǐn bāoyóu	phr.	free shipping of goods
3.	套装优惠	tàozhuāng yōuhuì	phr.	package discount
4.	买一送一	mǎi yī sòng yī	phr.	buy one and get one free
5.	设置免运门槛	shèzhì miǎn yùn ménkǎn	phr.	set a threshold for free shipping
6.	无门槛免运	wú ménkǎn miǎn yùn	phr.	no threshold for free shipping
7.	现金返还	xiànjīn fǎnhuán	phr.	cashback

第二部分 Part 2
汉字 Chinese Characters

一、汉字知识 Hànzì zhīshi Knowledge about Chinese Characters

1. 汉字的笔画（7） Strokes of Chinese characters (7)

笔画 Strokes	名称 Names	例字 Examples
㇉	竖折折钩 shùzhézhégōu	马
㇈	横斜钩 héngxiégōu	风

81

2. 汉字的结构（3） Structures of Chinese characters (3)

结构类型 Structure types	例字 Examples	结构图示 Illustrations
上下结构 Top-bottom structure	爸 节	
上中下结构 Top-middle-bottom structure	意	

二、汉字认读与书写　Hànzì rèndú yǔ shūxiě　The Recognition and Writing of Chinese Characters

认读下列词语，并试着读写构成词语的汉字。

Recognize the following words, and try to read and write the Chinese characters forming these words.

运费折扣　　商品包邮　　套装优惠

运			费			折			扣		
商			品			包			邮		
套			装			优			惠		

第三部分　Part 3　日常用语 Daily Expressions

❶ 麻烦你替我请个假。Máfan nǐ tì wǒ qǐng gè jià. Would you please ask for leave for me?
❷ 我被骗了。Wǒ bèi piàn le. I was cheated.
❸ 别着急。Bié zháojí. Don't worry./ Take it easy.

第四部分　Part 4　单元实训 Unit Practical Training

店铺促销　diànpù cùxiāo　Sales Promotion of Stores

实训目的 Training purpose

了解电商平台上店铺促销的方式，能够结合具体的物品进行适当的店铺促销。

To understand the ways of sales promotion of stores on e-commerce platforms, and be able to carry out appropriate sales promotion of stores combining specific goods.

实训组织 Training organization

每组三人，设定一个组长。

Three students in each group, with a group leader.

实训内容 Training content

❶ 学习电商平台上店铺促销的方式。

Learn the ways of sales promotion of stores on e-commerce platforms.

（1）搜索关键词"牙膏"。

Search the keyword "toothpaste".

（2）找出有折扣活动的牙膏，指出折扣展示位。

Find the toothpastes with discount activities, and point out the discount display locations.

（3）找出有优惠券的牙膏，指出优惠券展示位。

Find the toothpastes with coupons, and point out the coupon display locations.

（4）找出有运费折扣的牙膏，指出运费折扣展示位。

Find the toothpastes with freight discount, and point out the freight discount display locations.

❷ 班级内比赛，比较各种促销活动的异同，看哪一组的促销活动吸引的顾客最多，卖出的牙膏最多。

Compete within the class to compare the differences and similarities of different promotional activities, and see the promotional activity of which group can attract the most customers and sell the most toothpaste.

❸ 教师点评。

The teacher comments.

第五部分　Part 5

单元小结　Unit Summary

词语 cíyǔ Vocabulary

普通词语　General Vocabulary

1.	基础	jīchǔ	n.	basis
2.	觉得	juéde	v.	feel
3.	实惠	shíhuì	adj.	substantial
4.	首页	shǒuyè	n.	home page
5.	醒目	xǐngmù	adj.	eye-catching
6.	有利于	yǒulì yú	phr.	be beneficial to
7.	视线	shìxiàn	n.	line of vision/sight
8.	改变	gǎibiàn	v.	change
9.	主动	zhǔdòng	adj.	taking the initiative
10.	自动	zìdòng	adv.	automatically

词语 Vocabulary

11.	一定	yídìng	adj.	certain
12.	数量	shùliàng	n.	quantity
13.	从而	cóng'ér	conj.	thus

专业词语　Specialized Vocabulary

1.	折扣	zhékòu	n.	discount
2.	原价	yuánjià	n.	original price
3.	优惠券	yōuhuìquàn	n.	coupon
4.	领券	lǐng quàn	phr.	get a coupon
5.	抵扣	dǐkòu	v.	deduct
6.	减免	jiǎnmiǎn	v.	exempt and reduce

补充专业词语　Supplementary Specialized Vocabulary

1.	运费折扣	yùnfèi zhékòu	phr.	freight discount
2.	商品包邮	shāngpǐn bāoyóu	phr.	free shipping of goods
3.	套装优惠	tàozhuāng yōuhuì	phr.	package discount
4.	买一送一	mǎi yī sòng yī	phr.	buy one and get one free
5.	设置免运门槛	shèzhì miǎn yùn ménkǎn	phr.	set a threshold for free shipping
6.	无门槛免运	wú ménkǎn miǎn yùn	phr.	no threshold for free shipping
7.	现金返还	xiànjīn fǎnhuán	phr.	cashback

句子 Sentences

1. 折扣活动是在商品原价基础上打折，让顾客觉得更实惠。
2. 优惠券可以在顾客下单时自动抵扣、减免一定数量的金额，从而使顾客获得更实惠的价格。

8

Huódòng cèhuà
活动策划
Activity Planning

píngtái huódòng cèhuà
平台 活动 策划
Planning of Platform Activities

huìyuán fúwù
会员服务
Member Service

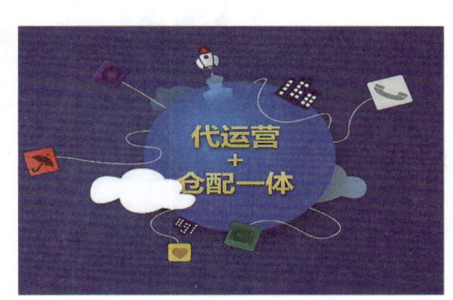

xìnxī fúwù
信息服务
Information Service

jiāoyì fúwù
交易服务
Transaction Service

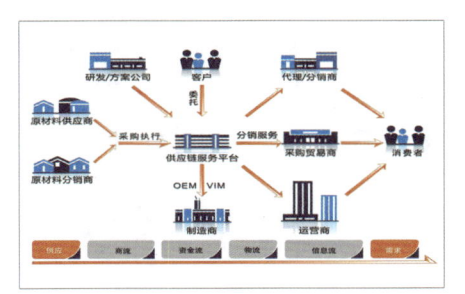

wùliú hé zījīnliú fúwù
物流和资金流服务
Logistics and Cash Flow Service

85

题解 Introduction

1. 学习内容：活动策划的类型和方法。
   Learning content: The types and ways of activity planning.
2. 知识目标：掌握与活动策划相关的关键词，学习汉字的笔画"乚""乁"和左右结构、左中右结构，学写本单元相关汉字。
   Knowledge objectives: To master the keywords related to activity planning, learn the strokes "乚", "乁", left-right structure and left-middle-right structure of Chinese characters, and write the characters related to this unit.
3. 技能目标：学会在电商平台上进行活动策划。
   Skill objectives: To learn to conduct activity planning on e-commerce platforms.

第一部分 Part 1

课文 Texts

一、热身 rèshēn Warm-up

1. 给词语选择对应的图片。 Choose the corresponding pictures for the words.

A. 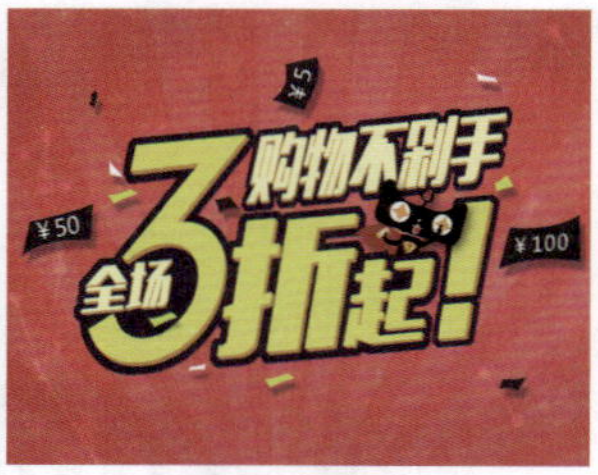　　　　　　　　B. 　　　　　　　　C. 　　　　　　　　D.

❶ zhékòu huódòng
  折扣 活动 _____
  discount activities

❷ jiérì huódòng
  节日 活动 _____
  festival activities

活动策划 8
Activity Planning

③ zhǔtí huódòng
主题活动 _____
theme activities

④ chǎnpǐn yōushì
产品优势 _____
product superiority

2. 看视频，了解平台活动的策划案例中需要考虑哪些因素，为相关视频选出正确的选项。
Watch the videos to learn factors that should be taken into consideration in platform activity planning cases, and choose the right options for the related videos.

pīngtái jīlì de huódòng cèhuà
平台激励的活动策划
Platform Inspired Activity Planning

A. huìyuán fúwù
会员服务
member service

B. xìnxī fúwù
信息服务
information service

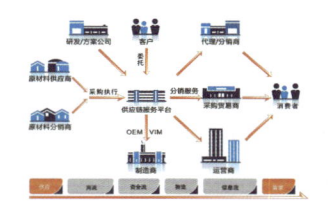

C. wùliú hé zījīnliú fúwù
物流和资金流服务
logistics and cash flow service

D. jiāoyì fúwù
交易服务
transaction service

① ▶ (   )   ② ▶ (   )   ③ ▶ (   )   ④ ▶ (   )

二、课文 kèwén Texts

A 🎧 08-01

Gēn diànzǐ shāngwù xiāngguān de jiérì yǒu hěn duō, rú "Shuāng Shíyī" Gòuwù Jié.
跟电子商务相关的节日有很多，如"双十一"购物节。
Zhèxiē jiérì wèi wǒmen huódòng cèhuà tígōngle biànlì, kěyǐ xīyǐn xiāofèizhě de zhùyì, tí-
这些节日为我们活动策划提供了便利，可以吸引消费者的注意，提
shēng wǎngdiàn de liúliàng, zēngjiā xiāoshòu'é.
升网店的流量，增加销售额。

87

中文 + 电子商务（中级）

译文 yìwén Text in English

There are many festivals related to e-commerce, such as "Double Eleven" shopping carnival. These festivals provide convenience for our activity planning to attract the attention of consumers, increase the traffic of online stores and their sales.

普通词语 pǔtōng cíyǔ General Vocabulary 🎧 08-02

1.	跟	gēn	prep.	with
2.	节日	jiérì	n.	festival
3.	多	duō	adj.	many, much
4.	如	rú	v.	give an example
5.	便利	biànlì	n.	convenience
6.	增加	zēngjiā	v.	increase

专业词语 zhuānyè cíyǔ Specialized Vocabulary 🎧 08-03

1.	双十一	Shuāng Shíyī	phr.	Double Eleven
2.	策划	cèhuà	v.	plan
3.	消费者	xiāofèizhě	n.	consumer
4.	网店	wǎngdiàn	n.	online store
5.	销售额	xiāoshòu'é	n.	sales

B 🎧 08-04

Huódòng cèhuà kǎolǜ de shǒuyào wèntí shì zhǔtí, yào shèjì yí gè xīyǐn xiāofèizhě
活动策划考虑的首要问题是主题，要设计一个吸引消费者

yǎnqiú de zhǔtí; qícì shì shèjì jùtǐ huódòng nèiróng, gěi xiāofèizhě tígōng duōyànghuà
眼球的主题；其次是设计具体活动内容，给消费者提供多样化

de huódòng xuǎnzé; zuìhòu shì shèzhì yìxiē shāngyè yíngxiāo shǒuduàn, jīlì xiāofèizhě gòumǎi.
的活动选择；最后是设置一些商业营销手段，激励消费者购买。

译文 yìwén Text in English

The primary consideration of activity planning is the theme, i.e., to design a theme that attracts the attention of consumers; secondly, to design specific activities to provide consumers with a wide variety of activity choices; finally, to set up some commercial marketing means to encourage consumers to buy.

普通词语 pǔtōng cíyǔ General Vocabulary 🎧 08-05

1.	首要	shǒuyào	adj.	primary
2.	主题	zhǔtí	n.	theme
3.	设计	shèjì	v.	design
4.	眼球	yǎnqiú	n.	eyeball
5.	其次	qícì	pron.	secondly, next
6.	具体	jùtǐ	adj.	concrete, specific
7.	给	gěi	prep.	for
8.	多样化	duōyànghuà	n.	diversification
9.	最后	zuìhòu	n.	the last
10.	一些	yìxiē	q.	some
11.	手段	shǒuduàn	n.	means

中文 + 电子商务（中级）

专业词语 zhuānyè cíyǔ Specialized Vocabulary			🎧 08-06
1. 商业	shāngyè	n.	commerce
2. 营销	yíngxiāo	v.	marketing
3. 购买	gòumǎi	v.	buy, purchase

三、视听说　shì-tīng-shuō　Viewing, Listening and Speaking

1. 看视频，了解电子商务平台在各大节日中活动策划的特点或方式，选择相关视频所描述的节日，并模仿说出电商平台活动策划的具体方式。

Watch the videos to learn about the characteristics or ways of activity planning of different festivals on e-commerce platforms, choose the festivals depicted in the related videos, and name specific ways of activity planning on e-commerce platforms following the videos.

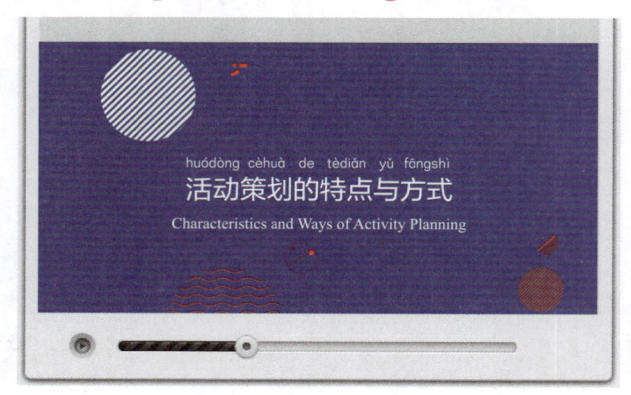

huódòng cèhuà de tèdiǎn yǔ fāngshì
活动策划的特点与方式
Characteristics and Ways of Activity Planning

Nǚshén Jié
A. 女神节
International Women's Day

"Shuāng Shíyī" Gòuwù Jié
B. "双十一"购物节
"Double Eleven" shopping festival

618 Gòuwù Jié
C. 618 购物节
618 shopping festival

Zhōngguó chuántǒng jiérì
D. 中国传统节日
traditional Chinese festivals

活动策划 **8**
Activity Planning

① ▶ (　　)　② ▶ (　　)　③ ▶ (　　)　④ ▶ (　　)

2. 说一说　Let's talk

模仿说出电商平台上节日活动的策划方式。　Name the methods of activity planning of festivals on e-commerce platforms following the videos.

四、学以致用　xuéyǐzhìyòng　Practicing What You Have Learnt

看视频，了解在电商平台上中国传统节日中适合的销售产品，并为相关视频选出正确的选项。
Watch the videos to learn about appropriate products for sale on traditional Chinese festivals on e-commerce platforms, and choose the right options for the related videos.

Duānwǔ Jié：zòngzi
A. 端午节：粽子
Dragon Boat Festival: rice dumplings

Zhōngqiū Jié：yuèbing
B. 中秋节：月饼
Mid-Autumn Festival: moon cakes, etc.

Chūnjié：jiǎozi
C. 春节：饺子
Spring Festival: dumplings

Yuánxiāo Jié：tāngyuán
D. 元宵节：汤圆
Lantern Festival: sweet dumplings

① ▶ (　　)　② ▶ (　　)　③ ▶ (　　)　④ ▶ (　　)

91

五、小知识 xiǎo zhīshi Tips

"双十一"购物节
"Shuāng Shíyī" Gòuwù Jié

"双十一"购物节，是指每年 11 月 11 日的网络促销日，源于淘宝商城（天猫）2009 年 11 月 11 日举办的网络促销活动。由于当天的营业额远超预想的效果，于是 11 月 11 日成为淘宝商城（天猫）举办大规模促销活动的固定日期。现在，"双十一"已成为中国电子商务行业的年度盛事，并且逐渐影响到国际电子商务行业。

"Double Eleven" Shopping Festival

The "Double Eleven" shopping festival refers to the online promotion day on November 11 every year, which was originated from the online promotion activity held by Taobao (Tmall) on November 11, 2009. The turnover of that day far exceeded expectation, so November 11 has become the fixed date for Taobao (Tmall) to hold large-scale promotion activities. Now "Double Eleven" has become an annual event for China's e-commerce industry and is gradually affecting the international e-commerce industry.

补充专业词语 bǔchōng zhuānyè cíyǔ Supplementary Specialized Vocabulary

1.	会员服务	huìyuán fúwù	phr.	member service
2.	信息服务	xìnxī fúwù	phr.	information service
3.	交易服务	jiāoyì fúwù	phr.	transaction service
4.	资金流服务	zījīnliú fúwù	phr.	cash flow service
5.	搜索量	sōusuǒliàng	n.	search volume
6.	预热活动	yùrè huódòng	phr.	warm-up activity
7.	购物津贴	gòuwù jīntiē	phr.	shopping coupon
8.	品类券	pǐnlèiquàn	n.	category coupon
9.	售卖	shòumài	v.	sell

第二部分 Part 2
汉字 Chinese Characters

一、汉字知识 Hànzì zhīshi Knowledge about Chinese Characters

1. 汉字的笔画（8） Strokes of Chinese characters (8)

笔画 Strokes	名称 Names	例字 Examples
ㄴ	竖弯 shùwān	四
ㄟ	横折弯 héngzhéwān	没

2. 汉字的结构（4） Structures of Chinese characters (4)

结构类型 Structure types	例字 Examples	结构图示 Illustrations
左右结构 Left-right structure	银 饭	⊟
左中右结构 Left-middle-right structure	班 微	⊞

二、汉字认读与书写 Hànzì rèndú yǔ shūxiě The Recognition and Writing of Chinese Characters

认读下列词语，并试着读写构成词语的汉字。
Recognize the following words, and try to read and write the Chinese characters forming these words.

狂欢节　消费者　销售额　搜索量

狂				欢				节				消			
费				者				销				售			
额				搜				索				量			

第三部分 Part 3
日常用语 Daily Expressions

❶ 你不能这样。Nǐ bù néng zhèyàng. You can't be like that.
❷ 我马上就到。Wǒ mǎshàng jiù dào. I will be there right away.
❸ 让我想想。Ràng wǒ xiǎngxiǎng. Let me think.

中文＋电子商务（中级）

第四部分　Part 4　单元实训 Unit Practical Training

电商平台活动策划　diànshāng píngtái huódòng cèhuà
Activity Planning of E-commerce Platforms

实训目的 Training purpose
了解电商平台节日活动的策划方法。
To learn about the methods of festival activity planning of e-commerce platforms.

实训组织 Training organization
每组两人，设定一个组长。
Two students in each group, with a group leader.

实训内容 Training content

❶ 学习电商平台"双十一"活动策划书的撰写。
　　Learn to draft an activity planning proposal for the "Double Eleven" of e-commerce platforms.

（1）活动背景："双十一"购物狂欢节，是指每年11月11日的网络促销日。
　　Activity background: the "Double Eleven" shopping carnival refers to the online promotion day on November 11th every year.

（2）活动报名："双十一"活动报名基本上在活动开始前1～2个月完成。
　　Activity registration: the registration of the "Double Eleven" activity is completed basically one or two months before the activity begins.

（3）定金支付：天猫要求报名"双十一"的商家一定要支付定金以保证平台及消费者利益。
　　Deposit payment: Tmall requires the sellers who have registered for the "Double Eleven" should pay the deposit to guarantee the benefits of the platform and consumers.

（4）活动主题：如"爱上时尚的'双十一'，国潮品牌折扣多多"。
　　Activity theme: for example, "fall in love with fashionable 'Double Eleven', plenty of discounts on Chinese fad brands".

（5）活动内容：如"单笔消费满200元减40元"。
　　Activity content: for example, "40 *yuan* off on a single purchase of 200 *yuan* or above".

（6）活动推广：内部推广和外部推广。
　　Activity promotion: internal promotion and external promotion.

❷ 班级内比赛，看哪一组做的活动策划书最好。
　　Compete within the class to see which group makes the best activity planning proposal.

❸ 教师点评。
　　The teacher comments.

第五部分　Part 5
单元小结　Unit Summary

词语 cíyǔ Vocabulary

普通词语　General Vocabulary

1.	跟	gēn	prep.	with
2.	节日	jiérì	n.	festival
3.	多	duō	adj.	many, much
4.	如	rú	v.	give an example
5.	便利	biànlì	n.	convenience
6.	增加	zēngjiā	v.	increase
7.	首要	shǒuyào	adj.	primary
8.	主题	zhǔtí	n.	theme
9.	设计	shèjì	v.	design
10.	眼球	yǎnqiú	n.	eyeball
11.	其次	qícì	pron.	secondly, next
12.	具体	jùtǐ	adj.	concrete, specific
13.	给	gěi	prep.	for
14.	多样化	duōyànghuà	n.	diversification
15.	最后	zuìhòu	n.	the last
16.	一些	yìxiē	q.	some
17.	手段	shǒuduàn	n.	means

专业词语　Specialized Vocabulary

1.	双十一	Shuāng Shíyī	phr.	Double Eleven
2.	策划	cèhuà	v.	plan
3.	消费者	xiāofèizhě	n.	consumer
4.	网店	wǎngdiàn	n.	online store
5.	销售额	xiāoshòu'é	n.	sales
6.	商业	shāngyè	n.	commerce
7.	营销	yíngxiāo	v.	marketing
8.	购买	gòumǎi	v.	buy, purchase

	补充专业词语		Supplementary Specialized Vocabulary		
cíyǔ 词语 Vocabulary	1.	会员服务	huìyuán fúwù	phr.	member service
	2.	信息服务	xìnxī fúwù	phr.	information service
	3.	交易服务	jiāoyì fúwù	phr.	transaction service
	4.	资金流服务	zījīnliú fúwù	phr.	cash flow service
	5.	搜索量	sōusuǒliàng	n.	search volume
	6.	预热活动	yùrè huódòng	phr.	warm-up activity
	7.	购物津贴	gòuwù jīntiē	phr.	shopping coupon
	8.	品类券	pǐnlèiquàn	n.	category coupon
	9.	售卖	shòumài	v.	sell

jùzi
句子
Sentences

1. 这些节日为我们活动策划提供了便利，可以吸引消费者的注意，提升网店的流量。
2. 活动策划考虑的首要问题是主题。
3. 其次是设计具体活动内容。
4. 最后是设置一些商业营销手段。

9

Yōuzhì kèfú
优质客服
High Quality Customer Service

yōuzhì kèfú
优质客服
High Quality Customer Service

jíshí huífù
及时回复
Respond in Time

zhēnzhèng jiějué wèntí
真正 解决 问题
Solve the Problem Genuinely

lǐmào
礼貌
Be Polite

97

题解　Introduction

1. 学习内容：电商客服的工作方式和工作流程。
   Learning content: The working manner and process of e-commerce customer service.
2. 知识目标：掌握与客服工作相关的关键词，学习汉字的笔画"ƷӠ""Ł"和全包围结构、半包围结构，学写本单元相关汉字。
   Knowledge objectives: To master the keywords related to customer service, learn the strokes "Ʒ", "Ł", fully-enclosed structure and semi-enclosed structure of Chinese characters, and write the characters related to this unit.
3. 技能目标：掌握客服的售前和售后服务流程。
   Skill objectives: To master the pre-sales and after-sales service processes of customer service.

第一部分　Part 1

课文　Texts

一、热身　rèshēn　Warm-up

1. 给词语选择对应的图片。　Choose the corresponding pictures for the words.

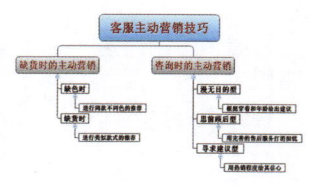

A.　　　B.　　　C.　　　D.

98

优质客服
High Quality Customer Service 9

① kèfú
客服 _____
customer service

② hǎopíng
好评 _____
positive review

③ chàpíng
差评 _____
negative review

④ huàshù
话术 _____
verbal trick

2. 看视频，了解并比较售前客服和售后客服的工作语言，把不同的客服类型与视频中的语言连线。
Watch the video to learn about and compare the working language of the pre-sales and after-sales customer services, and connect different types of customer services to the language in the video.

① shòu qián kèfú
售 前客服
pre-sales customer service

② shòu hòu kèfú
售 后客服
after-sales customer service

Nín hǎo, qǐngwèn shì xiǎng tuìhuò ma?
A. 您好，请问是想退货吗？
Hello, do you want to return the goods?

Qīn, xiǎng zīxún shénme?
B. 亲，想咨询什么？
My dear, what do you want to consult?

Qīn, duì zhè kuǎn liányīqún gǎn xìngqù ma?
C. 亲，对这款连衣裙感兴趣吗？
My dear, are you interested in this dress?

Nín hǎo, yǒu shénme bù mǎnyì de ma?
D. 您好，有什么不满意的吗？
Hello, do you have any complaints?

二、课文 kèwén Texts

A 09-01

Hǎo de shòu qián kèfú néng zēngjiā chǎnpǐn de xiāoliàng. Kuàisù、rèqíng de huífù kèhù
好的售前客服能增加产品的销量。快速、热情地回复客户

de wèntí, kěyǐ xiāochú kèhù de yílù, zēngjiā kèhù de xìnrèngǎn, chuándá chǎnpǐn de
的问题，可以消除客户的疑虑，增加客户的信任感，传达产品的

yōudiǎn, jìn'ér yǐndǎo kèhù xiàdān.
优点，进而引导客户下单。

译文 yìwén Text in English

Good pre-sales customer service can increase the sales volume of products. Responding to customers' questions quickly and enthusiastically can eliminate customers' doubts, enhance their trust, convey the merits of products, thus guiding customers to place orders.

普通词语 pǔtōng cíyǔ General Vocabulary 09-02

1.	热情	rèqíng	adj.	passionate
2.	回复	huífù	v.	respond
3.	消除	xiāochú	v.	eliminate
4.	疑虑	yílù	n.	doubt, suspicion
5.	信任感	xìnrèngǎn	n.	sense of trust
6.	传达	chuándá	v.	convey
7.	优点	yōudiǎn	n.	merit
8.	进而	jìn'ér	conj.	and then
9.	引导	yǐndǎo	v.	guide

专业词语 zhuānyè cíyǔ Specialized Vocabulary 09-03

1.	售前	shòu qián	phr.	pre-sales
2.	客服	kèfú	n.	customer service

B 09-04

Zài chǎnpǐn xiāoshòu de guòchéng zhōng, shòu hòu yě shì hěn zhòngyào de yì huán, xūyào
在产品销售的过程中，售后也是很重要的一环，需要
kèfú rényuán de jīngxīn chǔlǐ, bǐrú shuō wùliú chūle wèntí、dìngdān jiāoyì chūxiànle jiūfēn
客服人员的精心处理，比如说物流出了问题、订单交易出现了纠纷
děng. Yīncǐ, kèfú rényuán xūyào duì mǎijiā de shòu hòu wèntí zuòchū tuǒshàn de chǔlǐ.
等。因此，客服人员需要对买家的售后问题做出妥善的处理。

译文 yìwén Text in English

In the process of product sales, after-sales service is also a very important part, which requires careful handling of logistics problems, order transaction disputes, and other problems by customer service personnel. Therefore, customer service personnel need to properly deal with buyers' after-sales problems.

普通词语 pǔtōng cíyǔ General Vocabulary 09-05

1.	一环	yì huán	phr.	one link
	环	huán	n.	link
2.	精心	jīngxīn	adj.	careful, meticulous
3.	比如说	bǐrú shuō	phr.	for example
4.	出	chū	v.	happen
5.	妥善	tuǒshàn	adj.	proper, appropriate

专业词语 zhuānyè cíyǔ Specialized Vocabulary 09-06

1.	售后	shòu hòu	phr.	after-sales
2.	纠纷	jiūfēn	n.	dispute

三、视听说　shì-tīng-shuō　Viewing, Listening and Speaking

1. 看视频，学习电商客服使用的不同欢迎词，为相关视频选择正确选项。
Watch the videos to learn different welcoming speeches of e-commerce customer service staff, and choose the right options for the related videos.

A. Xiànzài xiǎo diàn yǒu yōuhuì huódòng,
现在小店有优惠活动，
qīnqīn yǒu shíjiān kěyǐ liǎojiě yíxiàr.
亲亲有时间可以了解一下儿。
Dear, we have special offers now.
You can take a look around if you have time.

B. Qīnqīn, yǒu shénme kěyǐ wèi nín xiàoláo de?
亲亲，有什么可以为您效劳的？
Honey! What can I do for you?

C. Qīn'ài dā, nín hǎo! Huānyíng guānglín ××××!
亲爱哒，您好！欢迎光临××××！
Dear, hello! Welcome to XXXX!

① ▶ (　　)　　② ▶ (　　)　　③ ▶ (　　)

优质客服 9
High Quality Customer Service

2. 说一说　Let's talk

模仿说出电商客服的欢迎词。　Name the welcoming speeches of e-commerce customer service following the videos.

四、学以致用　xuéyǐzhìyòng　Practicing What You Have Learnt

看视频，了解客服在沟通过程中存在的问题，给相关问题找出正确选项。
Watch the video to learn about the problems of customer service staff during the communication process, and choose the right options for the related problems.

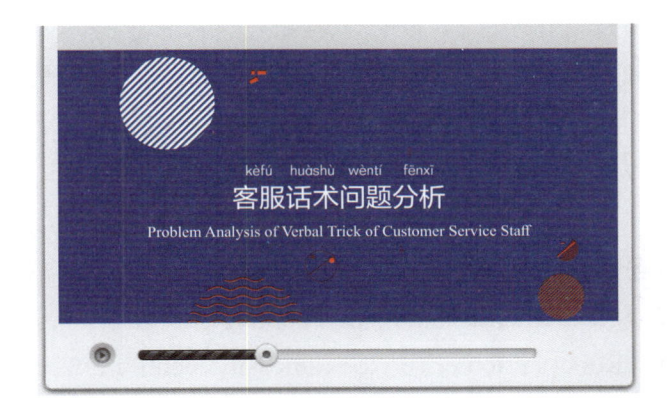

A.　　　　　　　B.　　　　　　　C.

❶ Bù jíshí huífù.
不及时回复。（　　）
Failing to respond in time.

❷ Fūyǎn, bù jiějué wèntí.
敷衍，不解决问题。（　　）
Being perfunctory and failing to solve the problem.

❸ Bù lǐmào.
不礼貌。（　　）
Being impolite.

103

五、小知识　xiǎo zhīshi　Tips

机器人客服
Jīqìrén kèfú

机器人客服是指利用人工智能（AI）等技术实现的人工智能客服，使得客服人员的时间能够用来解决更复杂的问题。机器人客服可以轻松识别不同类型的客户问询，擅长提供标准化的问题答案，目前已被广泛应用于电商行业。

Robot Customer Service

Robot customer service refers to artificial intelligence (AI) customer service that is realized by utilizing artificial intelligence (AI) and other technologies, enabling customer service staff to spend time solving more complex problems. Robot customer service can easily identify different types of customer inquiries and is good at providing standardized answers to questions. It has been widely used in the e-commerce industry now.

补充专业词语　bǔchōng zhuānyè cíyǔ　Supplementary Specialized Vocabulary　09-07

1.	优质客服	yōuzhì kèfú	phr.	high quality customer service
2.	好评	hǎopíng	n.	positive review
3.	差评	chàpíng	n.	negative review
4.	话术	huàshù	n.	verbal trick
5.	咨询	zīxún	v.	consult

第二部分　Part 2
汉字　Chinese Characters

一、汉字知识　Hànzì zhīshi　Knowledge about Chinese Characters

1. 汉字的笔画（9）Strokes of Chinese characters (9)

笔画 Strokes	名称 Names	例字 Examples
㇗	横折折撇 héngzhézhépiě	延、建
㇘	竖折撇 shùzhépiě	专

优质客服 9
High Quality Customer Service

2. 汉字的结构（5） Structures of Chinese characters (5)

结构类型 Structure types	例字 Examples	结构图示 Illustrations
全包围结构 Fully-enclosed structure	国	口
半包围结构 Semi-enclosed structure	医 边 问 唐 凶	

二、汉字认读与书写　Hànzì rèndú yǔ shūxiě　The Recognition and Writing of Chinese Characters

认读下列词语，并试着读写构成词语的汉字。
Recognize the following words, and try to read and write the Chinese characters forming these words.

热情回复　　消除疑虑　　传达优点

热			情			回			复		
消			除			疑			虑		
传			达			优			点		

第三部分　Part 3
日常用语　Daily Expressions

❶ 我该怎么办？ Wǒ gāi zěnme bàn? What shall I do?
❷ 麻烦你告诉我他的电话号码。Máfan nǐ gàosu wǒ tā de diànhuà hàomǎ. Would you please tell me his phone number?
❸ 真不好意思，我忘了给你打电话。Zhēn bù hǎoyìsi, wǒ wàngle gěi nǐ dǎ diànhuà. Sorry, I forgot to phone you.

第四部分 Part 4 单元实训 Unit Practical Training

电商优质客服　diànshāng yōuzhì kèfú　High Quality Customer Service

实训目的 Training purpose

了解电商客服售后工作的语言特点，学习其工作方式和工作流程。

To learn about language features of the after-sales work of e-commerce customer service reps, and learn their manner and process of working.

实训组织 Training organization

每组两人，一人演客户，一人演客服。

Two students in each group, with one as the customer and the other as the customer service rep.

实训内容 Training content

❶ 进行一段如下所示的售后对话。

　　Conduct an after-sales dialogue as the one below.

A：您好，亲爱哒！

　　Hello, dear!

Q：我想退掉这套运动装。

　　I'd like to return this suit of sportswear.

A：有什么让您不满意的吗？

　　Is there anything you are not satisfied with?

Q：这套衣服小了，我穿不了。

　　It is too small for me to wear.

A：我们可以帮您更换一套大的，可以吗？

　　We can change a bigger one for you, OK?

Q：可以。还有，运动装的包装袋破了。

　　That's fine. By the way, the packing bag of the sportswear is broken.

A：亲亲，请您拍照给我们，我们一定给您满意的答复。

　　Dear, please take a photo and send it to us, and we will give you a reply to your satisfaction.

Q：看到照片了吗？

　　Have you seen the photo?

A：嗯，对于快递公司给您带来的不便，我们非常抱歉。免费帮您更换可以吗？

　　Yes, we are very sorry for the inconvenience caused by the express company. We change it for you free of charge, OK?

Q：如果换了还是不合适，可以退吗？

　　If it is not fit after the change, can I return it?

A：您放心，七天无理由退换，可以退的。

　　Yes, please rest assured. You can return or change goods without giving any reason within seven days.

Q：好的，那怎么换？

OK. How to change it?

A：我把退换货流程发给您，麻烦您在线提交申请。

I'll send you the return and exchange process. Please submit your application online.

Q：好的，谢谢。

OK, thank you.

❷ 实训总结：客户评价客服服务。

Training summary: the customer comments on the service of the customer service rep.

❸ 教师点评。

The teacher comments.

第五部分 Part 5　单元小结 Unit Summary

词语 Vocabulary (cíyǔ)

普通词语　General Vocabulary

1.	热情	rèqíng	adj.	passionate
2.	回复	huífù	v.	respond
3.	消除	xiāochú	v.	eliminate
4.	疑虑	yílǜ	n.	doubt, suspicion
5.	信任感	xìnrèngǎn	n.	sense of trust
6.	传达	chuándá	v.	convey
7.	优点	yōudiǎn	n.	merit
8.	进而	jìn'ér	conj.	and then
9.	引导	yǐndǎo	v.	guide
10.	一环	yì huán	phr.	one link
	环	huán	n.	link
11.	精心	jīngxīn	adj.	careful, meticulous
12.	比如说	bǐrú shuō	phr.	for example
13.	出	chū	v.	happen
14.	妥善	tuǒshàn	adj.	proper, appropriate

专业词语　Specialized Vocabulary

1.	售前	shòu qián	phr.	pre-sales
2.	客服	kèfú	n.	customer service
3.	售后	shòu hòu	phr.	after-sales
4.	纠纷	jiūfēn	n.	dispute

补充专业词语　Supplementary Specialized Vocabulary

1.	优质客服	yōuzhì kèfú	phr.	high quality customer service
2.	好评	hǎopíng	n.	positive review
3.	差评	chàpíng	n.	negative review
4.	话术	huàshù	n.	verbal trick
5.	咨询	zīxún	v.	consult

cíyǔ 词语 Vocabulary

jùzi 句子 Sentences

1. 好的售前客服能增加产品的销量。
2. 快速、热情地回复客户的问题，可以消除客户的疑虑，增加客户的信任感，传达产品的优点，进而引导客户下单。
3. 在产品销售的过程中，售后也是很重要的一环，需要客服人员的精心处理。
4. 为防止买家给店铺差评，客服人员需要对买家的售后问题给出妥善的处理。

10 Yùnyíng shùjù fēnxī
运营数据分析
Operational Data Analysis

yùnyíng shùjù fēnxī
运营 数据分析
Operational Data Analysis

liúliàng yùnyíng shùjù fēnxī
流量 运营 数据分析
Data Analysis of Traffic Operations

nèiróng yùnyíng shùjù fēnxī
内容 运营 数据分析
Data Analysis of Content Operations

huódòng yùnyíng shùjù fēnxī
活动 运营 数据分析
Data Analysis of Activity Operations

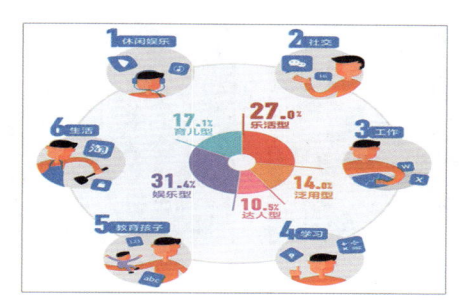

yònghù yùnyíng shùjù fēnxī
用户 运营 数据分析
Data Analysis of User Operations

中文 + 电子商务（中级）

> **题解　Introduction**
>
> 1. 学习内容：运营数据分析。
>   Learning content: Operational data analysis.
> 2. 知识目标：掌握与运营数据分析相关的关键词，复习汉字的笔画（总表）、笔顺（总表）和结构（总表），学写本单元相关汉字。
>   Knowledge objectives: To master the keywords related to operational data analysis, review the general tables of strokes, stroke orders and structures of Chinese characters, and write the characters related to this unit.
> 3. 技能目标：学会进行运营数据分析。
>   Skill objectives: To learn to conduct operational data analysis.

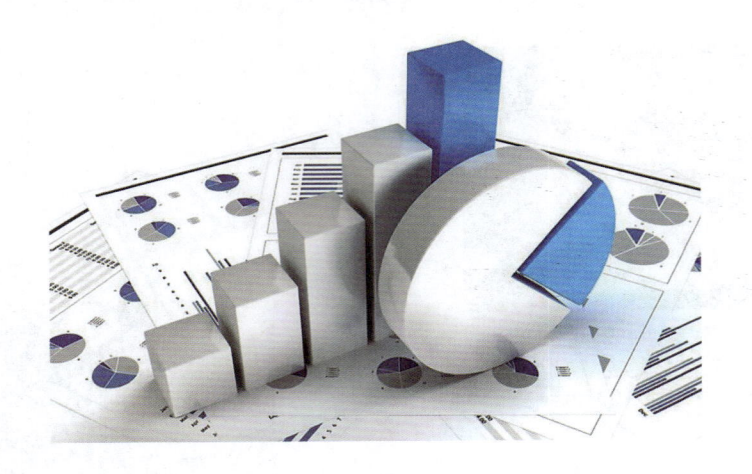

第一部分　Part 1

课文　Texts

一、热身　rèshēn　Warm-up

1. 给词语选择对应的图片。 Choose the corresponding pictures for the words.

A. 　　　　B. 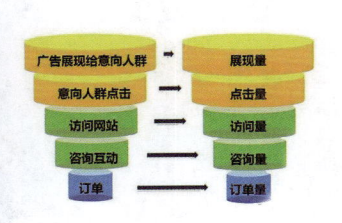　　　　C. 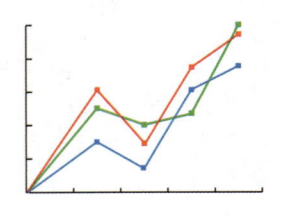　　　　D.

❶ zhuǎnhuàlǜ
　转化率_____
　conversion rate

❷ diǎnjīlǜ
　点击率_____
　click-through rate

110

运营数据分析 10
OPERATIONAL DATA ANALYSIS

③ zhǎnxiànliàng
展现量 _____
impression

④ zhéxiàntú
折线图 _____
line chart

2. 看视频，了解虾皮平台提供的商品分析功能，把选项标示在相应的红色框线旁。
Watch the video, get to know the goods analysis function provided by Shopee platform, and mark the options next to the corresponding red borders.

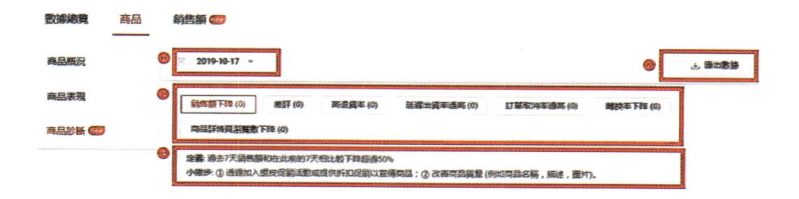

A. rìqī
日期
date

B. huìchū shùjù
汇出数据
exported data

C. zhěnduàn lèixíng
诊断 类型
diagnosis type

D. gǎijìn cèlüè
改进 策略
improvement strategy

二、课文　kèwén　Texts

A 🎧 10-01

Yùnyíng shùjù kěyǐ xiǎnshì shāngpǐn hé diànpù de xiāoshòu xìnxī. Fēnxī yùnyíng shùjù
运营 数据可以显示 商品 和店铺 的 销售 信息。分析运营 数据
kěyǐ fāxiàn yùnyíng guòchéng zhōng cúnzài de wèntí, jìn'ér tōngguò yùnyíng cèlüè jiějué
可以发现 运营 过程 中 存在的问题，进而 通过 运营 策略解决
wèntí, tíshēng diànpù liúliàng.
问题，提升 店铺 流量。

111

中文 + 电子商务（中级）

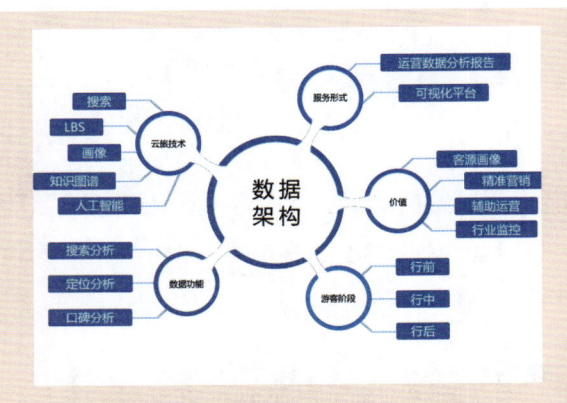

译文 yìwén Text in English

Operational data can show sales information of goods and stores. Through analysis of operational data, we can find problems in the operation process, and then solve the problems through operational strategies and increase store traffic.

普通词语 pǔtōng cíyǔ General Vocabulary 🎧 10-02

1.	分析	fēnxī	v.	analyze
2.	发现	fāxiàn	v.	discover
3.	存在	cúnzài	v.	exist
4.	解决	jiějué	v.	solve

专业词语 zhuānyè cíyǔ Specialized Vocabulary 🎧 10-03

1.	运营数据	yùnyíng shùjù	phr.	operational data
	数据	shùjù	n.	data
2.	运营策略	yùnyíng cèlüè	phr.	operational strategy
	策略	cèlüè	n.	strategy

B 🎧 10-04

Yùnyíng shùjù fēnxī ànlì: Tōngguò hòutái de xiāoshòu shùjù, wǒmen kěyǐ zhíjiē
运营数据分析案例：通过后台的销售数据，我们可以直接

chákàn shāngpǐn hé shāngjiā de zuì xīn xiāoshòu páimíng. Xiāoshòu zǒng'é shùjù kěyǐ chéngxiàn mài-
查看商品和商家的最新销售排名。销售总额数据可以呈现卖

jiā zài tèdìng shíjiān nèi de xiāoshòu zhuàngkuàng, bāokuò chūhuò dìngdān zài nèi de quánbù dìngdān.
家在特定时间内的销售状况，包括出货订单在内的全部订单。

运营数据分析 10
Operational Data Analysis

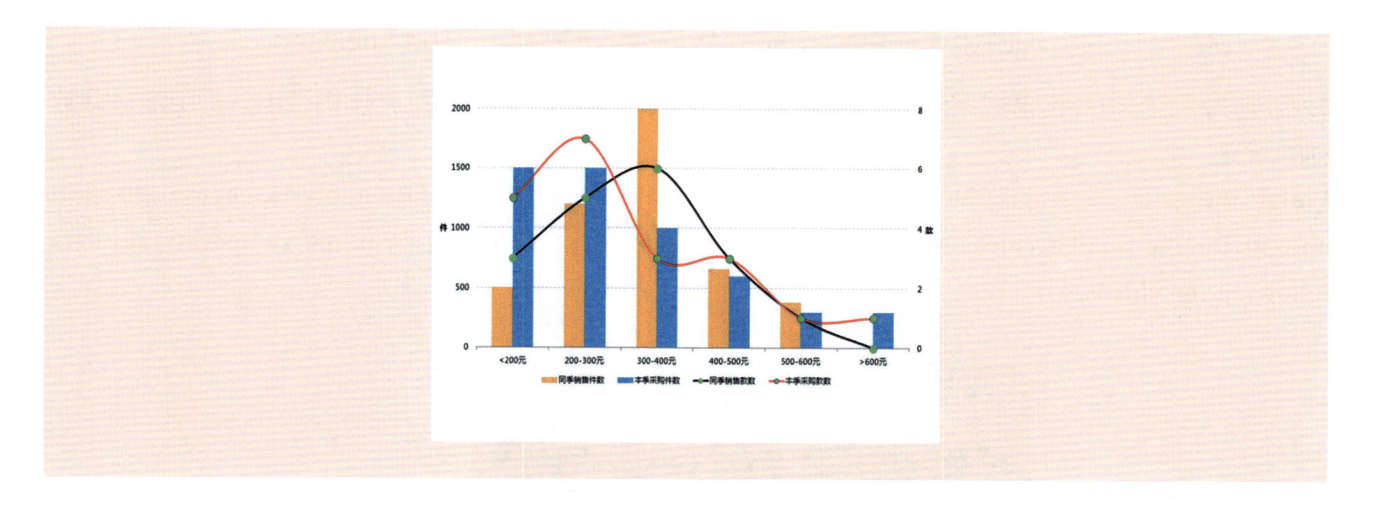

译文 yìwén Text in English

Case of operational data analysis: through the sales data at the back of the stage, we can directly view the latest sales ranking of goods and merchants. The total sales data can show the seller's sales situation in a specific period of time, and all orders including shipping orders.

普通词语 pǔtōng cíyǔ General Vocabulary 🎧 10-05

1.	后台	hòutái	n.	back of the stage
2.	直接	zhíjiē	adj.	direct
3.	新	xīn	adj.	new
4.	排名	pái//míng	v.	rank
5.	呈现	chéngxiàn	v.	show, appear
6.	特定	tèdìng	adj.	specific
7.	时间	shíjiān	n.	time
8.	状况	zhuàngkuàng	n.	condition, situation
9.	全部	quánbù	n.	all, whole

专业词语 zhuānyè cíyǔ Specialized Vocabulary 🎧 10-06

1.	总额	zǒng'é	n.	total amount
2.	出货订单	chūhuò dìngdān	phr.	shipping order
	出货	chū//huò	v.	take goods out of the warehouse

中文+电子商务（中级）

三、视听说　shì-tīng-shuō　Viewing, Listening and Speaking

1. 看视频，了解电商运营数据分析的类型，为相关视频选择正确的选项，并模仿说出分析电商运营数据的意义。

Watch the videos to learn about the types of e-commerce operational data analysis, choose the right options for the related videos, and talk about the meaning of analysing e-commerce operational data following the videos.

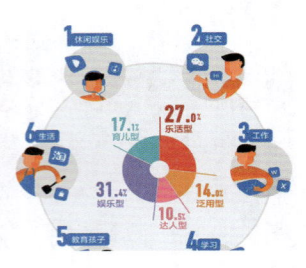

运营数据分析
yùnyíng shùjù fēnxī
Operational Data Analysis

A. liúliàng yùnyíng shùjù
流量 运营 数据
traffic operation data

B. huódòng yùnyíng shùjù
活动 运营 数据
activity operation data

C. nèiróng yùnyíng shùjù
内容 运营 数据
content operation data

D. yònghù yùnyíng shùjù
用户 运营 数据
user operation data

① ▶ (　　)　② ▶ (　　)　③ ▶ (　　)　④ ▶ (　　)

2. 说一说　Let's talk

模仿说出电商平台中运营数据分析的类型。**Name the types of operational data analysis of e-commerce platforms following the videos.**

运营数据分析
Operational Data Analysis 10

四、学以致用　xuéyǐzhìyòng　Practicing What You Have Learnt

看视频，学习电商平台上的运营数据分析图表，将正确选项填入图表中的相应位置。

Watch the video to learn the operational data analysis charts of e-commerce platforms, and fill the right options in the corresponding positions of the chart.

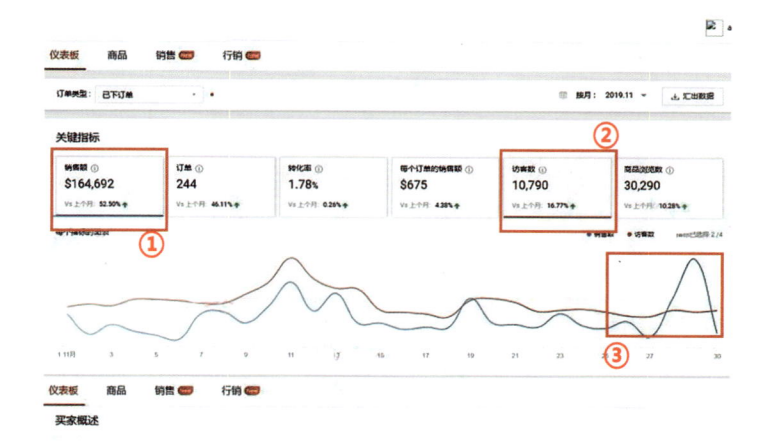

rènshi yùnying shùjù fēnxī túbiǎo
认识运营数据分析图表
Understand Operational Data Analysis Charts

　　　xiāoshòu'é zuì gāo diǎn
A. 销售额最高点
　　the highest point of sales

　　　gēn shàng gè yuè xiāngbǐ, xiāoshòu'é de zēngzhǎnglǜ
B. 跟上个月相比，销售额的增长率
　　growth rate of sales compared to last month

　　　gēn shàng gè yuè xiāngbǐ, fǎngkè shù de zēngzhǎnglǜ
C. 跟上个月相比，访客数的增长率
　　growth rate of visitors compared to last month

115

五、小知识 xiǎo zhīshi Tips

Diǎnjīliàng
点击量

Diǎnjīliàng shì zhǐ mǒu yí duàn shíjiān nèi mǒu gè guānjiàncí huòzhě túpiàn bèi diǎnjī de cìshù.
点击量是指某一段时间内某个关键词或者图片被点击的次数。
Zhǎnxiànliàng shì zhǐ yí duàn shíjiān nèi huòdé de zhǎnxiàn cìshù. Diǎnjīlǜ shì zhǐ bèi diǎnjī de
展现量是指一段时间内获得的展现次数。点击率是指被点击的
cìshù yǔ bèi xiǎnshì cìshù zhī bǐ. Zhuǎnhuàlǜ shì zhǐ gòumǎi rénshù yǔ fǎngkè rénshù zhī bǐ.
次数与被显示次数之比。转化率是指购买人数与访客人数之比。

Volume of Hits

Volume of hits refers to the number of times a certain keyword or picture is clicked within a certain period of time. Impression refers to the number of impressions obtained within a period of time. Click-through rate refers to the ratio of the number of clicks to the number of impressions. Conversion rate is the ratio of the number of purchasers to the number of visitors.

补充专业词语 bǔchōng zhuānyè cíyǔ Supplementary Specialized Vocabulary 🎧 10-07

1.	转化率	zhuǎnhuàlǜ	n.	conversion rate
2.	展现量	zhǎnxiànliàng	n.	impression
3.	折线图	zhéxiàntú	n.	line chart
4.	汇出数据	huìchū shùjù	phr.	exported data
5.	诊断类型	zhěnduàn lèixíng	phr.	diagnosis type
6.	改进策略	gǎijìn cèlüè	phr.	improvement strategy
7.	流量运营数据	liúliàng yùnyíng shùjù	phr.	traffic operation data
8.	用户运营数据	yònghù yùnyíng shùjù	phr.	user operation data
9.	内容运营数据	nèiróng yùnyíng shùjù	phr.	content operation data
10.	活动运营数据	huódòng yùnyíng shùjù	phr.	activity operation data
11.	增长率	zēngzhǎnglǜ	n.	growth rate

第二部分 Part 2

汉字 Chinese Characters

一、汉字知识　Hànzì zhīshi　Knowledge about Chinese Characters

1. 汉字的笔画（总表）　Strokes of Chinese characters (general table)

一	丨	丿	丶	丶	㇕	㇄
㇏	一	亅	丿	乚	㇀	㇚
㇉	㇄	㇙	㇄	丁	乙	㇌
㇋	㇆	㇈	㇊	㇉	乙	㇈

2. 汉字的笔顺（总表）　Stroke orders of Chinese characters (general table)

笔顺规则 Rules of stroke orders	例字 Examples
先横后竖	十
先撇后捺	人、八
先上后下	三
先左后右	人
先中间后两边	小
先外边后里边	问
先外后里再封口	国、日

3. 汉字的结构（总表）　Structures of Chinese characters (general table)

类型 Structure types	结构图示 Illustrations	例字 Examples
独体结构	☐	生、不
品字形结构	☐	品
上下结构	☐ ☐	爸、节
上中下结构	☐	意
左右结构	☐	银、饭
左中右结构	☐	班、微
全包围结构	☐	国
半包围结构	☐ ☐ ☐ ☐ ☐	医、边、问、唐、凶

中文 + 电子商务（中级）

二、汉字认读与书写　Hànzì rèndú yǔ shūxiě　The Recognition and Writing of Chinese Characters

认读下列词语，并试着读写构成词语的汉字。
Recognize the following words, and try to read and write the Chinese characters forming these words.

运营数据　　销售总额　　店铺流量

运			营			数			据		
销			售			总			额		
店			铺			流			量		

第三部分　Part 3　日常用语 Daily Expressions

❶ 谢谢你的礼物，我很喜欢。Xièxie nǐ de lǐwù, wǒ hěn xǐhuan. Thanks for your gift. I like it very much.

❷ 谢谢您的邀请，我一定去。Xièxie nín de yāoqǐng, wǒ yídìng qù. Thanks for your invitation. I will go for sure.

❸ 我该走了，再见。Wǒ gāi zǒu le, zàijiàn. I've got to go. Bye.

第四部分　Part 4　单元实训 Unit Practical Training

电商平台运营数据分析　diànshāng píngtái yùnyíng shùjù fēnxī
Operational Data Analysis of E-commerce Platforms

实训目的 Training purpose

了解电商平台需要分析哪些运营数据，能够了解并学会对运营数据进行分析和解读。

To understand what operational data e-commerce platforms need to analyze, and be able to understand and learn to analyze and interpret operational data.

实训组织 Training organization

每组三人，设定一个组长。

Three students in each group, with a group leader.

实训内容 Training content

❶ 各组选择处于初期、发展期及成熟期的三个卖家。

Each group selects three sellers in the early stage, development stage and mature stage.

（1）分析店铺初期订单、浏览量和转化率数据。

Analyze the data on orders, views and conversion rate of the store during its early stage.

（2）分析店铺发展期订单、浏览量和转化率数据。

Analyze the data on orders, views and conversion rate of the store during its development stage.

（3）分析店铺成熟期订单、浏览量和转化率数据。

Analyze the data on orders, views and conversion rate of the store during its mature stage.

❷ 根据数据帮助卖家增强对店铺的了解，并给出运营调整策略。

Based on the data, help the sellers enhance their understanding of the stores, and offer strategies for adjusting the operations.

❸ 小组进行汇报，展示分析的数据及提供的策略。

Each group makes a presentation, showing the analyzed data and the provided strategies.

❹ 教师点评。

The teacher comments.

第五部分　Part 5　单元小结　Unit Summary

词语 cíyǔ Vocabulary

普通词语　General Vocabulary

1.	分析	fēnxī	v.	analyze
2.	发现	fāxiàn	v.	discover
3.	存在	cúnzài	v.	exist
4.	解决	jiějué	v.	solve
5.	后台	hòutái	n.	back of the stage
6.	直接	zhíjiē	adj.	direct
7.	新	xīn	adj.	new
8.	排名	pái//míng	v.	rank
9.	呈现	chéngxiàn	v.	show, appear
10.	特定	tèdìng	adj.	specific
11.	时间	shíjiān	n.	time
12.	状况	zhuàngkuàng	n.	condition, situation
13.	全部	quánbù	n.	all, whole

cíyǔ 词语 Vocabulary

专业词语　Specialized Vocabulary

1.	运营数据	yùnyíng shùjù	phr.	operational data
	数据	shùjù	n.	data
2.	运营策略	yùnyíng cèlüè	phr.	operational strategy
	策略	cèlüè	n.	strategy
3.	总额	zǒng'é	n.	total amount
4.	出货订单	chūhuò dìngdān	phr.	shipping order
	出货	chū//huò	v.	take goods out of the warehouse

补充专业词语　Supplementary Specialized Vocabulary

1.	转化率	zhuǎnhuàlǜ	n.	conversion rate
2.	展现量	zhǎnxiànliàng	n.	impression
3.	折线图	zhéxiàntú	n.	line chart
4.	汇出数据	huìchū shùjù	phr.	exported data
5.	诊断类型	zhěnduàn lèixíng	phr.	diagnosis type
6.	改进策略	gǎijìn cèlüè	phr.	improvement strategy
7.	流量运营数据	liúliàng yùnyíng shùjù	phr.	traffic operation data
8.	用户运营数据	yònghù yùnyíng shùjù	phr.	user operation data
9.	内容运营数据	nèiróng yùnyíng shùjù	phr.	content operation data
10.	活动运营数据	huódòng yùnyíng shùjù	phr.	activity operation data
11.	增长率	zēngzhǎnglǜ	n.	growth rate

jùzi 句子 Sentences

1. 运营数据可以显示商品和店铺的销售信息。
2. 分析运营数据可以发现运营过程中存在的问题，进而通过运营策略解决问题，提升店铺流量。
3. 销售总额数据可以呈现卖家在特定时间内的销售状况。

附录 Appendices

词语总表 Vocabulary

序号	生词	拼音	词性	词义	普通G/专业S	所属单元
1.	案例	ànlì	n.	case	S	1A
2.	把	bǎ	prep.	used to put the object before the verb	G	5B
3.	包邮	bāoyóu	v.	ship for free	S	2A
4.	报备	bàobèi	v.	report	S	1A
5.	报名	bàomíng	v.	sign up	G	1A
6.	爆款	bàokuǎn	n.	hot-selling product	S	3A
7.	被	bèi	prep.	used in a passive sentence to introduce the agent/doer	G	1B
8.	比如说	bǐrú shuō	phr.	for example	G	9B
9.	必不可少	bìbùkěshǎo	phr.	essential, indispensable	G	3B
10.	便利	biànlì	n.	convenience	G	8A
11.	标题	biāotí	n.	title	S	4A
12.	表现	biǎoxiàn	v.	display, manifest	G	2A
13.	并	bìng	adv.	also	G	1A
14.	补贴	bǔtiē	n.	subsidy	S	2B
15.	不实定价	bù shí dìngjià	phr.	deceitful pricing	S	1
16.	才	cái	adv.	used to indicate that sth. happens only under certain conditions	G	3A
17.	参加	cānjiā	v.	join, take part in	G	1A
18.	参数	cānshù	n.	parameter	S	4
19.	参与	cānyù	v.	participate in	G	3B
20.	测试	cèshì	v.	test	S	5B
21.	策划	cèhuà	v.	plan	S	8A
22.	策略	cèlüè	n.	strategy	S	10A
23.	查看	chákàn	v.	check, inspect	G	5A
24.	差评	chàpíng	n.	negative review	S	9
25.	产品	chǎnpǐn	n.	product	S	3A
26.	成	chéng	v.	become	G	5B
27.	成为	chéngwéi	v.	become	G	2B
28.	呈现	chéngxiàn	v.	show, appear	G	10B
29.	惩罚	chéngfá	v.	punish	S	1B
30.	充值	chōngzhí	v.	top up	S	2

（续表）

31.	出	chū	v.	happen	G	9B
32.	出货	chū//huò	v.	take goods out of the warehouse	S	10B
33.	出货订单	chūhuò dìngdān	phr.	shipping order	S	10B
34.	出现	chūxiàn	v.	appear	G	5A
35.	处以	chǔ yǐ	phr.	be punished by	G	1B
36.	传达	chuándá	v.	convey	G	9A
37.	此	cǐ	pron.	this	G	2B
38.	从而	cóng'ér	conj.	thus	G	7B
39.	促销	cùxiāo	v.	promote sales	S	1A
40.	存在	cúnzài	v.	exist	G	10A
41.	达到	dádào	v.	reach	G	2B
42.	打造	dǎzào	v.	shape, make	S	3A
43.	大量	dàliàng	adj.	many, much	G	1A
44.	单纯	dānchún	adj.	pure, mere	G	6B
45.	当地	dāngdì	n.	locality	G	3A
46.	盗版	dàobǎn	n.	pirated edition	S	2
47.	地	de	part.	used after an adjective/a phrase to form an adverbial adjunct before the verb	G	2A
48.	抵扣	dǐkòu	v.	deduct	S	7B
49.	第	dì	pref.	a prefix indicating ordinal numbers	G	4B
50.	点	diǎn	m.	used in counting items	G	4B
51.	点击	diǎnjī	v.	click	G	6B
52.	点击率	diǎnjīlǜ	n.	click-through rate	S	4B
53.	店铺定位	diànpù dìngwèi	phr.	store orientation	S	3
54.	店铺权限	diànpù quánxiàn	phr.	store permission	S	1B
55.	定价	dìng//jià	v.	set a price	S	3B
56.	定位	dìngwèi	n.	orientation, niche	G	3A
57.	冻结账户资金	dòngjié zhànghù zījīn	phr.	freeze account funds	S	1
58.	对	duì	prep.	to	G	5A
59.	多	duō	adj.	many, much	G	8A
60.	多次	duō cì	phr.	many times	G	1B
61.	多样化	duōyànghuà	n.	diversification	G	8B
62.	恶意	èyì	n.	malice	G	1B
63.	发现	fāxiàn	v.	discover	G	10A
64.	反馈	fǎnkuì	v.	feedback	S	1A

(续表)

65.	返现	fǎnxiàn	v.	cashback	S	2A
66.	方面	fāngmiàn	n.	aspect	G	5B
67.	非法	fēifǎ	adj.	illegal	S	1
68.	费用	fèiyong	n.	expense	S	2A
69.	分	fēn	n.	point	G	2B
70.	分析	fēnxī	v.	analyze	G	10A
71.	封面图	fēngmiàntú	n.	cover image	S	5A
72.	付费	fùfèi	v.	pay	S	6A
73.	付费引流	fùfèi yǐnliú	phr.	paid traffic driving	S	6A
74.	付邮试用	fù yóu shìyòng	phr.	pay postage for product trial	S	6
75.	负面	fùmiàn	adj.	negative	S	1A
76.	改变	gǎibiàn	v.	change	G	7B
77.	改进策略	gǎijìn cèlüè	phr.	improvement strategy	S	10
78.	高	gāo	adj.	high	G	5B
79.	给	gěi	prep.	for	G	8B
80.	跟	gēn	prep.	with	G	8A
81.	更	gèng	adv.	more	G	2A
82.	功能	gōngnéng	n.	function	S	5B
83.	购买	gòumǎi	v.	buy, purchase	S	8B
84.	购物津贴	gòuwù jīntiē	phr.	shopping coupon	S	8
85.	关店	guān diàn	phr.	close a store	S	1A
86.	关键	guānjiàn	n.	key	G	3A
87.	关键词广告	guānjiàncí guǎnggào	phr.	keyword advertisement	S	3
88.	关联广告	guānlián guǎnggào	phr.	discovery advertisement	S	3
89.	关联营销	guānlián yíngxiāo	phr.	related marketing	S	6
90.	关停店铺	guān tíng diànpù	phr.	close a store	S	1
91.	官方旗舰店	guānfāng qíjiàndiàn	phr.	official flagship store	S	4
92.	广告	guǎnggào	n.	advertisement	S	3
93.	广告花费	guǎnggào huāfèi	phr.	advertising expenditure	S	6
94.	广告投放	guǎnggào tóufàng	phr.	advertisement serving	S	6
95.	过程	guòchéng	n.	process	G	1B
96.	好评	hǎopíng	n.	positive review	S	9
97.	合适	héshì	adj.	proper, right	G	3A
98.	后台	hòutái	n.	back of the stage	G	10B
99.	话术	huàshù	n.	verbal trick	S	9

（续表）

100.	环	huán	n.	link	G	9B
101.	环节	huánjié	n.	link	G	3B
102.	回复	huífù	v.	respond	G	9A
103.	汇出数据	huìchū shùjù	phr.	exported data	S	10
104.	会员服务	huìyuán fúwù	phr.	member service	S	8
105.	活动	huódòng	n.	activity	S	1A
106.	活动运营数据	huódòng yùnyíng shùjù	phr.	activity operation data	S	10
107.	获得	huòdé	v.	get	G	2B
108.	机会	jīhuì	n.	opportunity	G	2B
109.	基础	jīchǔ	n.	basis	G	7A
110.	激励	jīlì	v.	encourage	S	2A
111.	季节属性	jìjié shǔxìng	phr.	seasonal attribute	S	3A
112.	价格段	jiàgé duàn	phr.	price tier	S	2
113.	减免	jiǎnmiǎn	v.	exempt and reduce	S	7B
114.	简洁	jiǎnjié	adj.	concise	G	4B
115.	奖励	jiǎnglì	v.	reward	G	2A
116.	降低	jiàngdī	v.	lower	G	1B
117.	交易服务	jiāoyì fúwù	phr.	transaction service	S	8
118.	节日	jiérì	n.	festival	G	8A
119.	解决	jiějué	v.	solve	G	10A
120.	进而	jìn'ér	conj.	and then	G	9A
121.	禁卖商品	jìn mài shāngpǐn	phr.	prohibited goods	S	1
122.	精挑细选	jīngtiāo-xìxuǎn	phr.	carefully select	G	4B
123.	精心	jīngxīn	adj.	careful, meticulous	G	9B
124.	竞争力	jìngzhēnglì	n.	competitiveness	S	3A
125.	纠纷	jiūfēn	n.	dispute	S	9B
126.	具备	jùbèi	v.	have	G	3A
127.	具体	jùtǐ	adj.	concrete, specific	G	8B
128.	具有	jùyǒu	v.	have	G	3B
129.	决定	juédìng	v.	decide	G	4A
130.	觉得	juéde	v.	feel	G	7A
131.	看到	kàndào	phr.	see	G	4A
132.	考虑	kǎolǜ	v.	consider	G	3A
133.	可读性	kědúxìng	n.	readability	G	4B
134.	客服	kèfú	n.	customer service	S	9A

（续表）

135.	库存	kùcún	n.	stock	S	2
136.	快速	kuàisù	adj.	quick	G	4A
137.	款式	kuǎnshì	n.	style	S	5B
138.	利用	lìyòng	v.	utilize	G	6A
139.	联系	liánxì	v.	contact	G	1A
140.	了解	liǎojiě	v.	learn about, understand	G	4A
141.	领券	lǐng quàn	phr.	get a coupon	S	7B
142.	另外	lìngwài	conj.	besides	G	3B
143.	浏览者	liúlǎnzhě	n.	viewer	S	4A
144.	流行趋势	liúxíng qūshì	phr.	fashion trend	S	3
145.	流量	liúliàng	n.	traffic, volume of flow	S	4B
146.	流量运营数据	liúliàng yùnyíng shùjù	phr.	traffic operation data	S	10
147.	买家	mǎijiā	n.	buyer	S	1A
148.	买一送一	mǎi yī sòng yī	phr.	buy one and get one free	S	7
149.	卖点	màidiǎn	n.	selling point	S	4A
150.	卖点词	màidiǎncí	n.	selling point term	S	4A
151.	免	miǎn	v.	exempt	G	2A
152.	免费引流	miǎnfèi yǐnliú	phr.	free traffic driving	S	6A
153.	秒杀活动	miǎoshā huódòng	phr.	second kill	S	3
154.	名	míng	n.	name	G	4A
155.	明了	míngliǎo	adj.	clear	G	4B
156.	某	mǒu	pron.	some, certain	G	2B
157.	目标人群	mùbiāo rénqún	phr.	target group	S	3
158.	内	nèi	n.	within	G	2B
159.	内容	nèiróng	n.	content	G	5B
160.	内容运营数据	nèiróng yùnyíng shùjù	phr.	content operation data	S	10
161.	能	néng	aux.	can	G	3A
162.	能否	néngfǒu	v.	can or cannot	G	4A
163.	能够	nénggòu	aux.	can	G	4A
164.	排名	pái//míng	v.	rank	G	10B
165.	配饰	pèishì	n.	accessory	G	2B
166.	品类活动	pǐnlèi huódòng	phr.	category campaign	S	3
167.	品类券	pǐnlèiquàn	n.	category coupon	S	8
168.	评分	píngfēn	n.	grade, mark, score	G	2B
169.	评价	píngjià	n.	comment, review	S	1B

(续表)

170.	其次	qícì	pron.	secondly, next	G	8B
171.	其中	qízhōng	n.	among	G	2A
172.	潜质	qiánzhì	n.	potential	G	3A
173.	强	qiáng	adj.	strong, resolute	G	4B
174.	侵权	qīnquán	v.	infringe on sb.'s rights	S	1
175.	侵权风险	qīnquán fēngxiǎn	phr.	risk of infringement	S	1
176.	清晰	qīngxī	adj.	clear	G	5B
177.	取消	qǔxiāo	v.	cancel	G	1A
178.	权限	quánxiàn	n.	permission	S	1B
179.	全部	quánbù	n.	all, whole	G	10B
180.	却	què	adv.	yet	G	1A
181.	让	ràng	v.	let	G	4A
182.	热情	rèqíng	adj.	passionate	G	9A
183.	热搜词	rèsōucí	n.	hot search term	S	4A
184.	人气	rénqì	n.	popularity	G	6A
185.	如	rú	v.	give an example	G	8A
186.	辱骂买家	rǔmà mǎijiā	phr.	abuse buyers	S	1
187.	三	sān	num.	three	G	4B
188.	删除刊登商品	shānchú kāndēng shāngpǐn	phr.	delete published goods	S	1
189.	商店广告	shāngdiàn guǎnggào	phr.	store advertisement	S	3
190.	商家	shāngjiā	n.	business firm/company/person	S	2A
191.	商品包邮	shāngpǐn bāoyóu	phr.	free shipping of goods	S	7
192.	商业	shāngyè	n.	commerce	S	8B
193.	上新	shàng xīn	phr.	launch something new	S	2B
194.	设计	shèjì	v.	design	G	8B
195.	设置免运门槛	shèzhì miǎn yùn ménkǎn	phr.	set a threshold for free shipping	S	7
196.	声誉	shēngyù	n.	reputation	S	1A
197.	时	shí	n.	a period of time	G	4B
198.	时间	shíjiān	n.	time	G	10B
199.	时尚	shíshàng	n.	fashion	G	2B
200.	实惠	shíhuì	adj.	substantial	G	7A
201.	使用	shǐyòng	v.	use	G	5B
202.	市场	shìchǎng	n.	market	G	3A
203.	市场分析	shìchǎng fēnxī	phr.	market analysis	S	3

126

（续表）

204.	视线	shìxiàn	n.	line of vision/sight	G	7A
205.	是否	shìfǒu	adv.	whether... or not	G	4A
206.	收费	shōufèi	v.	charge	S	6B
207.	手段	shǒuduàn	n.	means	G	8B
208.	首要	shǒuyào	adj.	primary	G	8B
209.	首页	shǒuyè	n.	home page	G	7A
210.	售后	shòu hòu	phr.	after-sales	S	9B
211.	售卖	shòumài	v.	sell	S	8
212.	售前	shòu qián	phr.	pre-sales	S	9A
213.	输入	shūrù	v.	input	G	5A
214.	属于	shǔyú	v.	belong to	G	6A
215.	数据	shùjù	n.	data	S	10A
216.	数量	shùliàng	n.	quantity	G	7B
217.	刷	shuā	v.	brush	S	1B
218.	刷单	shuādān	v.	click farming	S	1B
219.	双十一	Shuāng Shíyī	phr.	Double Eleven	S	8A
220.	搜索	sōusuǒ	v.	search	S	4B
221.	搜索量	sōusuǒliàng	n.	search volume	S	8
222.	套装优惠	tàozhuāng yōuhuì	phr.	package discount	S	7
223.	特定	tèdìng	adj.	specific	G	10B
224.	特卖	tèmài	v.	sell at a special discount	S	2B
225.	提升	tíshēng	v.	promote	G	4B
226.	体验	tǐyàn	n.	experience	S	1A
227.	通常	tōngcháng	adv.	usually	G	4A
228.	同类	tónglèi	n.	of the same kind/category	G	3B
229.	突出	tūchū	v.	lay emphasis on	G	4B
230.	图文并茂	túwén-bìngmào	phr.	be excellent in both illustrations and texts	S	5
231.	推出	tuīchū	v.	release	G	2A
232.	推动	tuīdòng	v.	promote, push forward	G	2A
233.	推广	tuīguǎng	v.	promote	S	2A
234.	妥善	tuǒshàn	adj.	proper, appropriate	G	9B
235.	网店	wǎngdiàn	n.	online store	S	8A
236.	为了	wèile	prep.	for the sake of, in order to	G	2A
237.	文案	wén'àn	n.	copy	S	5B
238.	无门槛免运	wú ménkǎn miǎn yùn	phr.	no threshold for free shipping	S	7

(续表)

239.	吸引	xīyǐn	v.	attract	G	3B
240.	细节	xìjié	n.	detail	S	5B
241.	细节图	xìjiétú	n.	detail image	S	5
242.	显示	xiǎnshì	v.	display	S	6B
243.	现金返还	xiànjīn fǎnhuán	phr.	cashback	S	7
244.	限时	xiànshí	v.	limit the time	S	2B
245.	限制账户权限	xiànzhì zhànghù quánxiàn	phr.	limit account permissions	S	1
246.	相关	xiāngguān	v.	be related to	G	5A
247.	详情页	xiángqíngyè	n.	detail page	S	5A
248.	享有	xiǎngyǒu	v.	enjoy (rights/fame/prestige)	G	2B
249.	消除	xiāochú	v.	eliminate	G	9A
250.	消费习惯	xiāofèi xíguàn	phr.	consumption habit	S	3A
251.	消费者	xiāofèizhě	n.	consumer	S	8A
252.	销量	xiāoliàng	n.	sales volume	S	1B
253.	销售额	xiāoshòu'é	n.	sales	S	8A
254.	效果	xiàoguǒ	n.	effect	S	5B
255.	新	xīn	adj.	new	G	10B
256.	信任感	xìnrèngǎn	n.	sense of trust	G	9A
257.	信息服务	xìnxī fúwù	phr.	information service	S	8
258.	信息过载	xìnxī guòzài	phr.	information overload	S	5
259.	型号	xínghào	n.	model	S	4
260.	醒目	xǐngmù	adj.	eye-catching	G	7A
261.	虚假产品	xūjiǎ chǎnpǐn	phr.	fake product	S	1
262.	需要	xūyào	v.	need, demand	G	3A
263.	许多	xǔduō	num.	many, much	G	2A
264.	选出	xuǎnchū	phr.	select	G	3A
265.	选品	xuǎn pǐn	phr.	product selection	S	3A
266.	眼球	yǎnqiú	n.	eyeball	G	8B
267.	一定	yídìng	adj.	certain	G	7B
268.	疑虑	yílǜ	n.	doubt, suspicion	G	9A
269.	以下	yǐxià	n.	the following	G	4B
270.	一般	yìbān	adj.	general, ordinary	G	6A
271.	一环	yì huán	phr.	one link	G	9B
272.	一些	yìxiē	q.	some	G	8B

(续表)

273.	因	yīn	prep.	because of	G	1A
274.	因素	yīnsù	n.	element, factor	G	3A
275.	引导	yǐndǎo	v.	guide	G	9A
276.	引流	yǐnliú	v.	drive traffic	S	3B
277.	印象	yìnxiàng	n.	impression	G	5A
278.	营销	yíngxiāo	v.	marketing	S	8B
279.	影响	yǐngxiǎng	v.	affect	G	1A
280.	用户	yònghù	n.	user	S	6B
281.	用户运营数据	yònghù yùnyíng shùjù	phr.	user operation data	S	10
282.	佣金	yòngjīn	n.	commission	S	2A
283.	优点	yōudiǎn	n.	merit	G	9A
284.	优化	yōuhuà	v.	optimize	S	4B
285.	优惠券	yōuhuìquàn	n.	coupon	S	7B
286.	优势	yōushì	n.	advantage	G	3B
287.	优选	yōuxuǎn	v.	optimize	S	2B
288.	优质客服	yōuzhì kèfú	phr.	high quality customer service	S	9
289.	有利于	yǒulì yú	phr.	be beneficial to	G	7A
290.	与	yǔ	prep.	with	G	1A
291.	预热活动	yùrè huódòng	phr.	warm-up activity	S	8
292.	预算设定	yùsuàn shèdìng	phr.	budget setting	S	6
293.	欲望	yùwàng	n.	desire	G	5A
294.	原价	yuánjià	n.	original price	S	7A
295.	原因	yuányīn	n.	reason	G	1A
296.	月	yuè	n.	month	G	2B
297.	运费	yùnfèi	n.	freight	S	2B
298.	运费折扣	yùnfèi zhékòu	phr.	freight discount	S	7
299.	运营策略	yùnyíng cèlüè	phr.	operational strategy	S	10A
300.	运营数据	yùnyíng shùjù	phr.	operational data	S	10A
301.	造成	zàochéng	v.	result in	G	1A
302.	增加	zēngjiā	v.	increase	G	8A
303.	增长	zēngzhǎng	v.	increase	G	2A
304.	增长率	zēngzhǎnglǜ	n.	growth rate	S	10
305.	展示	zhǎnshì	v.	show, present	G	5B
306.	展现量	zhǎnxiànliàng	n.	impression	S	10
307.	站内	zhàn nèi	phr.	on-site	G	6A

（续表）

308.	折扣	zhékòu	n.	discount	S	7A
309.	折线图	zhéxiàntú	n.	line chart	S	10
310.	这样	zhèyàng	pron.	this way, such	G	3A
311.	诊断类型	zhěnduàn lèixíng	phr.	diagnosis type	S	10
312.	政策	zhèngcè	n.	policy	G	2A
313.	直接	zhíjiē	adj.	direct	G	10B
314.	只有	zhǐyǒu	conj.	only	G	3A
315.	中	zhōng	n.	inside, being within a certain range/sphere	G	1B
316.	种	zhǒng	m.	kind, type	G	2A
317.	重要	zhòngyào	adj.	important	G	3B
318.	主动	zhǔdòng	adj.	taking the initiative	G	7B
319.	主题	zhǔtí	n.	theme	G	8B
320.	主图	zhǔtú	n.	main image	S	5B
321.	注意	zhùyì	v.	pay attention to	G	4B
322.	转化率	zhuǎnhuàlǜ	n.	conversion rate	S	10
323.	状况	zhuàngkuàng	n.	condition, situation	G	10B
324.	咨询	zīxún	v.	consult	S	9
325.	资金流服务	zījīnliú fúwù	phr.	cash flow service	S	8
326.	资源位	zīyuánwèi	n.	resource-niche	S	2A
327.	自动	zìdòng	adv.	automatically	G	7B
328.	自己	zìjǐ	pron.	one's own, oneself	G	1A
329.	总额	zǒng'é	n.	total amount	S	10B
330.	总共	zǒnggòng	adv.	altogether, in total	G	2B
331.	最	zuì	adv.	most	G	5B
332.	最后	zuìhòu	n.	the last	G	8B
333.	做	zuò	v.	make	G	5B

附录
Appendices

视频脚本　Video Scripts

第一单元　虾皮处罚规则

一、热身
禁止在平台买卖的货品

虾皮网上不允许售卖枪支、弹药、军火及仿制品。虚假产品评价也是不允许的。国家保护类植物活体禁止在虾皮网上售卖。用于非法摄像、录音、取证等用途的设备禁止在虾皮网上售卖。

三、视听说
了解电商处罚规则

视频① A：我知道使用未认证的第三方软件也会被处罚。
　　　　B：是的，如果还在短时间内就上传了大量商品就会被处罚。
视频② A：千万不要辱骂买家，或者对买家有过激的语言。
　　　　B：是的，服务态度必须好，否则会被处罚。
视频③ A：电商有哪些商品不能销售？
　　　　B：不要卖假货或者有侵权风险的商品。
视频④ A：网上什么商品都能销售吗？
　　　　B：当然不是，售卖平台都有明文规定的禁卖商品以及限制商品。

四、学以致用
关于处罚规则的案例

视频① 小机器人：大家好！今天我来和大家聊一聊几种处罚规则，大家判断一下儿这些店家都违反了什么处罚规则。店家A为了吸引顾客，将2980块的电视机定价为1298元，让大家进行抢购。
视频② 店家B本来卖的是羊肉，可是他却把关键字输入成牛肉。
视频③ 店家C的商品品种不够，他就把仅有的十种货品每隔一段时间再重复上架。
视频④ 店家D打着广告卖名牌包，可是全都不是真正的名牌。

第二单元　激励政策

一、热身
电商平台激励政策

视频① Shopee平台免费直播推广两次。
视频② 店铺可免费参与CCB返点活动，为期两周。
视频③ 运费降一半，实效不打折。
视频④ 买家可以使用Shopee币抵现。

三、视听说
电商卖家激励政策的条件

视频① A：重物渠道店铺当月上新量达到200，可以获得激励吗？
　　　　B：可以的，如果其他条件也符合，就可以获得一级奖励。
视频② A：汽摩用品目标类目上新达到300，可以获得激励吗？
　　　　B：可以的，如果其他条件也符合，就可以获得一级奖励。
视频③ A：汽摩用品目标类目上新达到200，可以获得激励吗？

131

B：可以的，如果其他条件也符合，就可以获得新卖家奖。
视频④ A：重物渠道店铺当月上新量达到100，可以获得激励吗？
B：可以的，如果其他条件也符合，就可以获得二级奖励。

四、学以致用
有关虾皮平台的激励政策等级

小机器人：大家好！今天我来和大家聊一聊几种获得激励政策的条件及相应等级的激励政策。店家A入驻时间在两到三个月，可以获得非新商家的激励。店家B店铺评分达到4.2分，要综合考虑入驻时间进行判断。店家C店铺一个月内上新达到50，可以获得新卖家激励。店家D是新店，上新产品符合目标价格要求，获得新卖家激励。

第三单元　爆款打造

一、热身
爆款打造的流程
助理：主管，我们怎么打造爆款？
主管：爆款打造主要分四个步骤：选择合适的产品，产品要有卖点；优化产品标题和主图；定价，价格要有吸引力；要对产品进行促销推广。

三、视听说
选择产品的关注事项
视频① 选品时要选质量好、款式新、有卖点、顾客愿意买的产品。
视频② 选择产品要考虑季节和当下的流行趋势。比如夏季要选择夏装，食品要选绿色健康的。
视频③ 要根据店铺定位和目标人群的喜好来选择产品，面向年轻人的运动鞋店铺要选择新款的鞋子来打造爆品。
视频④ 卖家选品前要做市场分析，了解当地人的消费习惯。比如在印度，当地人不用筷子，所以筷子是成不了爆款的。

四、学以致用
促销活动和广告推广

小机器人：大家好！虾皮平台上有很多的促销活动，平时定期会举行品类活动，比如男装折扣活动，还有一年一度的"双十一"大促以及各种秒杀活动。品类活动要求低，新店铺可以多参加，提升流量和曝光率。虾皮上的付费广告主要分为关键词广告、关联广告和商店广告三种。关联广告和店铺广告对销量和店铺等级有要求，新店铺可以先设置关键词广告。

第四单元　标题优化

一、热身
认识产品标题

第一个产品标题，售卖的是鞋子，品牌是李宁，产品名是跑步鞋。第二个产品标题，售卖的是电脑，品牌是华为，产品名是笔记本电脑。第三个产品标题，售卖的是手机，品牌是华为，产品名是手机。第四个产品标题，售卖的是包，品牌是爱迪生，产品名是书包。

三、视听说
标题优化技巧
A：标题里可以放与产品无关的热搜词吗？
B：不可以，标题里的关键词要与产品高度相关。
A：关键词要不要选择热搜词？
B：要的，与产品相关的热搜词能够让产品更容易被买家搜索到。

A：哪些关键词能吸引点击率？
B：关键词要突出卖点，才能吸引买家，从而提高成交量。
A：选择关键词还有什么要注意的吗？
B：关键词应该简洁明了，不要有无效关键词。

四、学以致用
标题优化技巧

　　小机器人：大家好！我们来看一看这个手机标题是由哪些部分组成的。"Xiaomi/小米 Note 10"是手机的品牌和名称。"8＋128G"是手机的参数，8G 的运行内存和 128G 的机身存储。"新品""全面屏"，还有"送碎屏险"是这款手机的卖点。"智能手机"和"学生手机"是热搜词。

第五单元　主图优化

一、热身
认识主图

　　电商平台上展示产品主要信息的图片叫作主图。虾皮上最多上传九张产品主图。第一张主图叫封面图。主图不仅可以上传图片，也可以上传视频。主图优化是为了吸引买家，提升点击率。

三、视听说
选择主图的原则

主图要清晰，一定要突出产品。文案要简洁，不能信息过载。主图要突出产品卖点，图文并茂。

四、学以致用
选择主图

　　小机器人：大家好！今天我来和大家聊一聊产品主图需要展示给买家的内容。如果我是帽子卖家，我的帽子主图里首要清晰地呈现帽子的外观和功能，让买家了解帽子的样子以及它的防晒功能；还要尽可能把帽子所有的款式和颜色都展示出来，让买家知道有更多的选择。另外，细节和使用效果也很重要，买家通过细节图可以全面了解帽子每个部位的设计以及做工质量，再加上真人佩戴的效果图，买家会更容易下单。

第六单元　站内引流

一、热身
站内引流的方式

视频① 设置店内热卖宝贝的链接。
视频② 付邮费进行产品的试用。
视频③ 大型促销活动。
视频④ 设置其他相关商品推荐的链接。

三、视听说
电商站内引流的广告方式

视频① A：关键词广告是站内引流广告的一种方式，是吗？
　　　　B：是的，为广告设置关键词，通过搜索引擎可以找到。
视频② A：关联广告是站内引流广告的一种方式，是吗？
　　　　B：是的，它是根据商品的相似性进行推荐的一种广告。
视频③ A：店铺广告是站内引流广告的一种方式，是吗？
　　　　B：是的，它是在店铺中展示的一种广告。

四、学以致用
站内引流广告的投放操作

小机器人：大家好！今天我来和大家聊一聊站内引流广告的使用方式。首先要对广告账户进行充值，广告使用前要先预热，然后开始运用广告提升销量，广告投入后，要监控广告成效。

第七单元　店铺促销

一、热身
店铺促销方式

视频① 运费折扣。

视频② 商品包邮。

视频③ 套装优惠。

视频④ 买一送一。

三、视听说
运费折扣促销

视频① 卖家在设置运费时直接设置为0，即商品无门槛包邮。只要买家买东西，就可以享受包邮政策，由商家承担运费。

视频② 卖家在设置运费时设置部分地区包邮。当买家的一个订单金额达到卖家设置的满减门槛，才能享受免运。

四、学以致用
虾皮店铺优惠券

视频① 小机器人：大家好！今天我来和大家聊一聊虾皮店铺的几种优惠券，大家根据图片的类型进行相关分类。虾皮优惠券的折扣可以分为三种，一种是固定折扣（如：满200送30等）。

视频② 一种是百分比折扣（如：50%等）。

视频③ 一种是硬币现金返还（如：满500返还现金50等）。

第八单元　活动策划

一、热身
平台激励的活动策划

视频① 会员服务。

视频② 信息服务。

视频③ 交易服务。

视频④ 物流和资金流服务。

三、视听说
活动策划的特点与方式

视频① 三八女神节（妇女节）期间，"康乃馨""首饰""丝巾""包包"等商品词的搜索量都有明显的上升。

视频② "双十一"拥抱主题活动策划，在11月11日光棍节策划情侣拥抱活动。

视频③ 618购物节前期有预热活动，如购物津贴、品类券等。

视频④ 中国传统节日注重传统商品的售卖，如端午节可以销售中国传统粽子、咸鸭蛋等产品。

四、学以致用
了解中国传统节日中适合的销售产品

视频① 小机器人：大家好！今天我来和大家聊一聊电商平台上关于传统节日中适合的销售产品，大家根据视频和图片的类型进行相关分类。端午节：粽子、打糕、咸鸭蛋等。

视频② 中秋节：月饼、桂花酒、田螺等。

视频③ 元宵节：汤圆、花灯、灯谜等。
视频④ 春节：饺子、年糕、鱼、面条儿等。

第九单元　优质客服

一、热身
售前客服和售后客服的工作语言
售前客服：亲，想咨询什么？亲，对这款连衣裙感兴趣吗？
售后客服：您好，有什么不满意的吗？您好，请问是想退货吗？

三、视听说
电商客服的话术
视频① 亲爱哒，您好！欢迎光临"××××"！请问有什么需要帮助的吗？
视频② 亲亲，有什么可以为您效劳的？
视频③ 亲，现在小店有优惠活动哦，亲亲有时间可以了解一下哦。

四、学以致用
客服话术问题分析
　　小机器人：大家好！今天我来和大家聊一聊客服在与客人沟通的过程中存在的问题，大家根据图片的类型进行相关分类。在沟通过程中存在的问题有很多种，现在列举出下面三种：一种是客服未能及时回复；一种是客服的态度很敷衍，不想或不能真正解决问题；一种是虽然在答复，但不太礼貌。

第十单元　运营数据分析

一、热身
商品分析功能
　　小机器人：虾皮平台提供了商品分析功能。日期表示数据的截止时间。汇出数据可以用图表显示数据。诊断类型中可以看到商品的各种数据分析，在改进策略中通过小提示提供改进方法。

三、视听说
运营数据分析
视频① A：流量运营数据分析属于电商数据分析吗？
　　　　B：是的，流量数据分析主要是为了促进流量的转化。
视频② A：内容运营数据分析属于电商数据分析吗？
　　　　B：是的，它是展示产品内容的数据分析，可以展示产品对用户的吸引度。
视频③ A：活动运营数据分析属于电商数据分析吗？
　　　　B：是的，它可以显示出活动的推广与销售效果。
视频④ A：用户运营数据分析属于电商数据分析吗？
　　　　B：是的，用户运营数据分析的目的是让用户活跃起来。

四、学以致用
认识运营数据分析图表
　　小机器人：大家好！今天我来和大家聊一聊运营数据分析图表内容，图中的两条线，蓝色表示销售额，红色表示访问量。在关键指标处可以看到销售额比上个月的增长率、访客数比上个月的增长率、订单数量和转化率、销售额最高点等信息。

参考答案 Reference Answers

第一单元

一、1.①A ②D ③C ④B
　　2.①C ②D ③A ④B
三、①B ②D ③A ④C
四、①C ②B ③D ④A

第二单元

一、1.①B ②A ③D ④C
　　2.①②③④
三、①A ②D ③C ④B
四、①C D ②A

第三单元

一、1.①B ②D ③C ④A
　　2.③②①④
三、①D ②C ③A ④B
四、B D

第四单元

一、1.①C ②A ③D ④B
　　2.①B ②C ③A ④D
三、①√ ②× ③√ ④×
四、上：A B B，下：D C B

第五单元

一、1.①D ②A ③C ④B
　　2.①√ ②√ ③× ④√
三、B
四、① ② ③ ④
　　A　B　C　D
（①-C, ②-A, ③-D, ④-B）

第六单元

一、1.①A ②B ③C ④D
　　2.①C ②D ③B ④A
三、①A ②C ③B
四、D A C B

第七单元

一、1.①A ②C ③B ④D
　　2.①A ②B ③D ④C

三、①B ②A
四、①C ②B ③A

第八单元

一、1.①B ②A ③D ④C
　　2.①A ②B ③D ④C
三、①A ②B ③C ④D
四、①A ②B ③D ④C

第九单元

一、1.①B ②A ③C ④D
　　2.①BC ②AD
三、①C ②B ③A
四、①C ②A ③B

第十单元

一、1.①B ②A ③C ④D
　　2.①A ②B ③C ④D
三、①A ②C ③B ④D
四、①B ②C ③A